LAUGHTER IN THE RAIN

NEIL SEDAKA

LAUGHTER IN THE RAIN

MY OWN STORY

G. P. PUTNAM'S SONS / NEW YORK

The author gratefully acknowledges permission from the following sources
to reprint material in their control:
  Screen Gems-EMI Music Inc., 6255 Sunset Blvd., Hollywood, CA
90028, for "Oh Carol" by Neil Sedaka and Howard Greenfield, copyright ©
1959 by Screen Gems-EMI Music Inc.; for "Oh Neil" by Neil Sedaka,
Howard Greenfield and Gerry Goffin, copyright © 1960 by Screen Gems-
EMI Music Inc.; and for "Breaking Up Is Hard to Do" by Neil Sedaka and
Howard Greenfield, copyright © 1962 and 1970 by Screen Gems-EMI
Music Inc. Used by permission. All rights reserved.
  Steinberg Music Co., 919 Third Avenue, New York, NY 10022, for "Sol-
itaire" by Neil Sedaka and Phil Cody, copyright © 1972, 1975 by Kiddio
Music Co., Top Pop Music Co., & Welbeck Music Co.; for "Our Last Song
Together" by Neil Sedaka and Howard Greenfield, copyright © 1973, 1974
by Kiddio Music Co.; for "The Immigrant" by Neil Sedaka and Phil Cody,
copyright © 1974, 1975 by Kiddio Music Co., Top Pop Music Co. & Welbeck Music Co.; and for "Laughter in the Rain" by Neil Sedaka and Phil
Cody, copyright © 1974 by Kiddio Music Co., Top Pop Music Co., & Welbeck Music Co. International copyright secured. All rights reserved.

Library of Congress Cataloging in Publication Data

  Sedaka, Neil.
  Laughter in the rain.

  1. Sedaka, Neil. 2. Singers—United States—
Biography. 3. Composers—United States—Biography.
I. Title.
ML410.S4443A3 1982   784.5′0092′4 [B]   82-11263
ISBN 0-399-12744-5

My special thanks go to
Ellis Amburn for his work,
his understanding, and
his gentle nature.

*To the memory of my
father, Mac Sedaka.*

CONTENTS

9

CONTENTS

APPENDIXES

Strolling along country roads with my baby,
It starts to rain, it begins to pour.
Without an umbrella we're soaked to the skin,
I feel a shiver run up my spine,
I feel the warmth of her hand in mine.

Oo, I hear laughter in the rain,
Walking hand in hand with the one I love.
Oo, how I love the rainy days
And the happy way I feel inside.

After a while we run under a tree,
I turn to her and she kisses me.
There with the beat of the rain on the leaves,
Softly she breathes and I close my eyes,
Sharing our love under stormy skies.

Oo, I hear laughter in the rain,
Walking hand in hand with the one I love.
Oo, how I love the rainy days
And the happy way I feel inside.

FOREWORD

There was a mind-boggling four-year period early in rock 'n' roll—'59-'62—when I had ten Top Ten records in a row with sales totaling over 25 million copies. I was speeding down the King's Highway in Brooklyn in my brand-new baby-blue T-bird convertible with the radio blaring my latest hit, "Oh, Carol," inspired by my steady girlfriend, Carole King, who'd later hit it big with "Will You Still Love Me Tomorrow." Connie Francis had launched me by recording a song I'd written, "Stupid Cupid," and after that I wrote a string of hit records, "Breaking Up Is Hard to Do," "Next Door to an Angel," "Where the Boys Are," and "Calendar Girl." As my buddy Bobby Darin said to me over coffee at Hanson's one day, "Baby, your mother may still control your bank account, but, face it, you're rock 'n' roll royalty."

Then, suddenly, as if waking from a dream, it was over. I couldn't give a song away. I had thought I'd be resilient enough to survive disaster, but when it came I was devastated. When The Beatles revolutionized pop music in the early '60's, many of the early rock stars were instantly obsolete. I wondered if I'd ever make it to the top again and the only consoling thought I had was, "Life's a roller coaster ride. Brace for another climb."

No wonder roller coasters have always haunted me. When my mother was pregnant, she tried to abort me by riding the Cyclone on Coney Island.

I refused to budge.

Later, growing up in Brooklyn, I would walk to Coney by myself in the winter months when it was cold and lonely. The rides were closed. I'd climb onto the tracks of the L.A. Thompson, a smaller coaster, and walk the length of the track, climbing slowly up and down the wooden hills and around the turns.

In the summer I'd ride the Tornado and the Bobsled, savoring the feeling of falling, that dropping sensation in the pit of your stomach, the screams of the riders as the wind blows in your face, the abrupt turns and sudden spurts of speed.

My life too has had its fast turns, its brief summits and sudden pitfalls. It has been a life strangely influenced by the sudden turns of a career of songwriting and performing. The roller coaster, like entertaining, is an escape from the ordinary.

For a short while the performer and the audience are thrown into a fantasy world. A world of laughter and rain.

PART I

MAKE-BELIEVE BALLROOM

1939–1956

CHAPTER 1
THE IMMIGRANT

Eleanor Sedaka tried every roller coaster in Coney Island in their order of ferocity: The Tornado, The Bobsled, The Virginia Reel, The Thunderbolt and the monstrous Cyclone. She was three months pregnant and was trying to abort the child—me.

Eleven months before, my sister Ronnie had struggled into the world and it had been such a desperate pregnancy that her doctor told Eleanor Sedaka, "No more children."

Fortunately Mom's attempts at aborting me were a big flop. On March 13, 1939, I was born in Madison Park Hospital, Brooklyn, New York.

Mom had been orphaned at the age of four, and her sister Annette was separated from the rest of the family. Mom and her two brothers, Carl and Sydney, were raised by their grandmother. There was never much money, and Mom had to work throughout most of her childhood. She was a petite seventeen-year-old when she met taxi driver Mac Sedaka one Saturday night at a social club on Ocean Parkway. Both Mom and Dad had given me verbatim accounts of this momentous event in their lives.

Eleanor was dancing with one of her favorite partners when Mac Sedaka strode up and cut in. Holding her close as he swept her away to the strains of "I'm in the Mood for Love," Mac said, "Why, you're light as a feather and twice as graceful. How much do you weigh?

"Eighty-four pounds. May I ask what you do?"

"I drive a cab, Skinny. Do you mind if I call you Skinny?"

Mac and Skinny danced the rest of the evening and he drove her home to Brooklyn in his Checker Cab.

Eleanor wasn't drawn to the personable cabbie sexually but she permitted Mac a goodnight kiss and the promise of dates to come.

Mac was a Sephardic Jew whose parents had immigrated from Turkey to settle on Manhattan's Lower East Side. Mom was an Ashkenazic Jew of Russian-Polish descent and called Mac "a black Jew" when she discussed him with her brother Sydney during their courtship.

"Mac's head over heels in love with you," Sydney said. "Has he proposed to you yet?"

"I'm not in love with Mac," Eleanor said.

"He has a steady job, Eleanor. Any girl in the neighborhood would jump at the chance to marry a man like Mac Sedaka."

Eleanor said, "These black Jews—I don't even speak their language. How am I going to know what my in-laws are saying about me if they're always kvetching in Ladino?"

"You're a practical one. I know you'll make the right decision, Eleanor."

Eleanor shrugged. "I've dreamed of having a strong, reliable man take care of me. Well, here's my big chance in life, staring me in the face. I'll *learn* to love Mac Sedaka."

Mac picked Eleanor up in his big cab one mild June evening in 1936 and took her to his railroad flat. On the fire escape two stories above the leisurely strollers—and scurrying rats—of Hester Street, Mac pulled Eleanor into a steamy embrace and won his dream girl.

Their marriage on July 4, 1936, was the standard Sephardic stampede. The Ashkenazi princess hissed to Sydney, "I didn't realize that every black Jew in Brooklyn was going to be invited."

The reception was held in a neighbor's two-family house. In a scorching 102° heat, family and friends shoved their way in, carrying covered dishes as wedding gifts—doughy pastries filled with cheese and meat, concoctions of beans and rice, and an array of tomato dishes. The newlyweds had to begin married life with only $12 in cash gifts. As the party progressed the house began to overflow and suddenly someone screamed, "Oy vay, the floor's caving in! Everybody out!" Guests dashed for the door, dinner plates in hand. The Royal Wedding this was not.

Neither was the honeymoon. Mom's brother Sydney and his new wife Syd came along and the two couples shared a single room in the LeRoy Hotel in Lock Sheldrake, New York. Sydney was broke and Mac's $12 had to cover everything.

Home was a small apartment on Voorhies Avenue in Brooklyn. Eleanor picked up Ladino on her own, asking thousands of questions, driving relatives crazy by interrupting their Ladino conversations to demand English translations.

In the midst of her struggles with this difficult language, Eleanor attended a big Sephardic Jewish affair during the High Holy Days at temple. The bride set out to impress everyone with her knowledge of Ladino. For days she practiced the phrase *anos mucho*—have many years—in front of the mirror until at last she was ready. Standing at the entranceway to the temple after the ceremony, she completely blew it by saying to each person as they left, "*Medio juevo*." Later she asked Mac why everyone was staring at her in horror. "Oh God, Skinny. You got your phrases mixed up. You meant *anos muchos*. '*Medio juevo*' means half a testicle. Skinny, you're a character!"

The first baby came on September 4, 1937—my sister Ronnie. Now they needed more space but were too poor to afford a large apartment. Mac's parents, Marie and Nisim, said, "Come!" even though they already had a full house. Four of my father's sisters, Kate, Molly, Ann and May, were already jammed into their two-bedroom apartment at 3260 Coney Island Avenue, sharing the rent.

I grew up in this tiny warren with nine people, doubling and sometimes quadrupling up to sleep. Mom, Dad, Ronnie and I slept in the big bedroom. Grandpa and Norni—Grandma in Ladino—took the little bedroom. The living room, which had a bright linoleum floor, contained Ann and May in one bed and Molly and Kate in another. These were some of the happiest years of my life—seven women, all taking care of me, Baby Nisimico.

Eleanor and Norni cooked Sephardic dishes with names like *yapracas*, *desayano* and *bureca*. Norni would cook for an entire day and the food would last out the week, congealing in a greasy, smelly pot and reheated each day. We would sit down to this sloppy goulash and eat with gusto. It was fatty and tasty thanks to quantities of salt, pepper, stewed tomatoes, onions and garlic. Much as I love my Norni, I suspect her goulash led to my stomach problems later in life. It's a fact that Grandpop expired from "overeating" when I was three.

Grandpop's death seemed like a big party to me. The Sephardic funeral is a grand ritual and feast. Norni spread a white bed sheet on the floor, and the mourners sat down and gorged themselves on hard-boiled eggs, olives and *yapracas*—stuffed grape leaves.

All the love that Eleanor Sedaka missed in her childhood she showered on Ronnie and me. The fact that she was not in love with her husband never bothered her. She had two children to devote her life to. It was she who wore the pants in the family and made all the decisions. Mac was a gentle and passive soul. Peace in the home was his priority and Mac was content to let his wife run the show. One thing Skinny couldn't convince him of, though, was to buy his own taxi medallion, which cost $35. Twenty years later it was worth $35,000. "I don't want the headaches and responsibilities of owning my own cab," he argued.

CHAPTER 2

SOLITAIRE'S THE ONLY GAME IN TOWN

I hated the first music I heard. Norni played some Turkish records she'd brought from the old country. They scared the hell out of me, but they reminded Norni of home and she played them repeatedly. I finally fled to the bathroom to escape the racket. But when Aunt Molly started bringing home American *placas*—records—I couldn't stop playing them and would listen for hours. They hooked me on music for life. Mom says I wouldn't eat until she put a *placa* on the Victrola.

The first record I bought was The Moylen Sisters, a popular group of the Forties. Mom took me—I was all of three—to a shop on the Kings Highway and I was so excited by the time we got home I slipped while running to the Victrola, fell on the linoleum, and shattered the 78 platter. I cried bitterly until Eleanor, ever the good Jewish mama, not wanting her baby crestfallen, rode the trolley back to Kings Highway and bought another 78 of The Moylen Sisters. This time she placed it on the turntable herself.

On April 12, 1945, I looked out the window and saw my mother crying as she hung clothes out to dry. I ran out to her and she took me in her arms, hugged me, and explained that President Franklin Delano Roosevelt had died. Although I didn't understand, I cried too. All of Brighton Beach was in mourning that day.

I grew up on the music of World War II. Sitting at the radio for hours at a time I'd listen to Bing Crosby, The Andrews Sisters, Kate Smith, and the Big Bands. Glenn Miller's "Chattanooga Choo-Choo" was my favorite. I used to make up my own Patty Andrews show before going to bed, commandeering my poor sister Ronnie to play Maxine. The only time I had to shut off the music was during WWII air raid blackouts.

In 1946, the pioneer disc jockey program, Martin Bloch's *Make Believe Ballroom*, was still an innovative radio show. Bloch made it seem as if the singers and bands were playing live in the studio. It was exhilarating.

My favorite singers were Les Paul and Mary Ford, Patti Page, Rosemary Clooney, Guy Mitchell, Kay Starr and the inimitable Johnnie Ray. I didn't know whether Johnnie Ray was a man or a woman but that didn't stop me from trying to imitate him. In fact, I sang along with all of them. I would have been disgraced if someone had come into the living room and caught me singing a perfect soprano.

Brighton Beach was a unique section of Brooklyn. In the 1940s it was a lower-to-middle class Jewish neighborhood where everyone looked the same and talked the same, families spoke Yiddish at home, had no contact with other neighborhoods, and thought the whole world was Jewish. I wouldn't lay eyes on a WASP for months at a time.

Summers, Brighton turned into an ocean resort with people coming from all over the city to sunbathe. They'd pour out of the last stop on the BMT subway line and head for the public beaches, miles of sand and ocean with a boardwalk that stretched from Manhattan Beach to Brighton Beach to Coney Island.

My family split their time between the public beach and the Brighton Beach Private Baths. The Baths was classier and involved an admission fee. There were paddle tennis courts, dancing, a cafeteria and concrete walks with wooden beach chairs, as well as three swimming pools filled with salt water. At night we would stroll on the boardwalk and watch the fireworks at 9 P.M. every Tuesday that lasted for a quarter of an hour. The other big entertainment on the boardwalk was people-watching. All the *yentas*—gossips—would sit on their beach chairs and watch the passing parade. They loved to note who was with whom, what people were wearing and where they were going.

The boys of Brighton were tough kids who learned to street fight at an early age, though they had to be respectful to their elders and behave themselves at home. Their main interests were baseball, stickball, kick the can, stoopball and running bases.

By the time I was ready to begin school, I realized I

was different from the other kids. I just didn't fit in
with guys like the fat kid who was the neighborhood
tough and his sidekicks.

Part of the problem was that I never had any friends.
My only companions were my sister, Mom, my
aunts—and my music. My father's hours as a cab
driver, working nights and supporting a family of four,
were absolutely killing. Somehow he found the time to
take me to Ebbets Field to see the Dodgers for a 60¢
ticket. He was a simple, thoughtful man and when he
realized I liked to watch prize fights he took me to box-
ing matches whenever he could. He'd also ride the Virginia Reel at Coney Island with me. Poppa urged me to
hang out with the guys, but when I brought a new
chum home to play one Saturday afternoon, Norni said
"*Mandalo!*—"Get rid of him."

I had no trouble making friends with the girls in
school, and I came to idealize my sister Ronnie as a
kind of goddess. We played together, slept in the same
room, became an inseparable pair. I would make her
sing songs with me, imitating the latest hit records,
pretending we were performers.

Mom never let me do anything for myself. I was a
poor eater and my family used to call me Too-Thin
Johnny.

Mom fed me every meal until I was *seven*, trying to
get me to put on weight.

"You need this, Nisimico," she said at the table. Despite my protests she mashed my potatoes and peas together, coaxing them down me. As a result I grew up
hating vegetables and fruit.

When Mom enrolled me in P.S. 253, which was

about two and a half blocks away, she refused to let me cross the street alone and accompanied me to class.

My first day of kindergarten we had an apple bobbing contest. I nearly drowned in the tub of water and later in the day puked from the apple peel. I had never eaten an apple peel before. Everyone laughed at me.

"You walk and talk like a girl," said the neighborhood tough.

By the first grade I was known as the school sissy. My first fight occurred during that year. A big ugly punk picked a fight with me and beat me to a pulp. When I came home with bruises, cuts and a torn shirt, my mother was aghast.

"What happened to you?" she asked frantically.

I explained about the fight. Her next question threw me.

"What condition is the other kid in?"

"He's in pretty bad shape," I lied, and my mother smiled hopefully.

Actually, he didn't have a scratch on him. I decided then that this would be my last fight. I knew I didn't have the size or strength to beat the older boys, and I realized I would have to use my head and talk my way out of fights. I also had to do something to make myself less different from the others.

The first step was to practice walking and gesturing in a masculine fashion in front of the mirror. I learned to carry my books under my arm instead of hugging them against my chest, as I had seen Ronnie do. Eventually the kids started ignoring me—what a relief.

Mom and Ronnie were of no help in this dilemma. They continued to shelter and baby me. If it rained I wasn't allowed to go to school for fear I would catch cold.

At last I made two friends. Freddie Gershon was a chubby kid who lived in the neighborhood, and we'd play paddle tennis at the Baths. He was my only male companion. The rest of the time I'd play potsie, jump rope and jacks with Carol Gold, the girl next door. Carol and I would go to the backyard and play our kind of ball games, as I was not accepted by the boys in the baseball games. I learned to be very good at handball and King—Chinese handball—which took less strength and more skill. I never did learn how to play baseball.

The destruction of my ego was well underway. I was a troubled child headed for a tragic, empty life.

CHAPTER 3

MUSES BY THE NAME OF GLANTZ AND GREENFIELD

I was mesmerized by Mrs. Glantz when she conducted the class choir. This warm, big-boned Brooklyn second-grade school teacher suddenly became a regular Leopold Stokowski. So commanding was her take-charge attitude that even Brooklyn toughs behaved when she lifted her baton.

Mrs. Glantz held the key to my destiny. She was the first to sense my musical aptitude. She could hear my voice above the others and eventually this perceptive and compassionate woman put me in front of the class choir to conduct. I was seven years old.

"Neil," Mrs. Glantz said, her eyes gleaming behind her rimless glasses, "you conduct with the flair of a *musician*."

It surprised me, and the class too. That was the first

time I saw admiration for something I had done in the faces of children my own age, and I suddenly realized I liked being admired.

"The class sissy is going to be someone special," I thought.

Mrs. Glantz gave me a letter to carry home to Mom: "Neil has real talent as a musician. I can tell already that he would be an exceptional pianist if given the opportunity. Is there any way that you could make a piano available to Neil? It would be so wonderful to see him develop his talent." Mom was delirious with joy. "My baby has talent!" she exclaimed, folding Mrs. Glantz's letter carefully. She took a part-time job for six months in a department store to earn the money for the piano, a second-hand upright she found for $500. Ronnie was dismayed to learn she was expected to take piano lessons as well.

"It just isn't right for Neil to take lessons alone," Mom said.

Murray Newman of Brighton Beach was my first piano teacher. "You have a natural facility for the piano," he told me. I was on Book Six of the John Thompson series within six months, while Ronnie was still laboring over Book One. Freddie Gershon began to take lessons, too.

I spent so much time practicing, Mom had to bring my meals to the piano. Family and friends dropped in to hear us play. My performances were oohed and aahed over; poor Ronnie's were politely acknowledged.

"But she's such a *pretty* girl, Eleanor," people would say. Even Aunt Freda, Aunt Minnie and Uncle Joey—

the music mavens—said of me, "Eleanor, he's a genius. We have another Martha in the family."

Martha, my maternal grandmother, had studied piano with the famous Walter Damrosch. She died at the age of twenty-eight, leaving four children. Her husband, too, was reputed to be a musician. Staggering under the shock of Martha's untimely death, he abandoned the children and supposedly went into show business as a singer under the name Farmer Miller. Aunt Freda also claimed that he invented the slide projector and wrote the song, "Let a Smile Be Your Umbrella," selling the rights for $25. Aunt Freda had a tendency to exaggerate.

After a few years, Murray Newman said there was nothing more he could teach me. He suggested that I audition for Juilliard Preparatory Division for Children, which had classes every Saturday. Mom and I, along with Freddie Gershon and his mother Miriam, took the subway to Juilliard at 122nd Street and Broadway to apply. Both Freddie and I were accepted and we began classes in 1947. I received a piano scholarship. By some clerical error, Freddie's piano teacher and mine were switched. I wound up with Edgar Roberts, a magnificent teacher for children, and Freddie ended up with Francis Goldstein, who was a tough cookie.

The Saturday routine at Juilliard consisted of a piano lesson followed by instruction in music literature and theory. Periodically, we had to give concerts in the auditorium in front of our parents, teachers and fellow students. Freddie, for his first concert, played a Scarlatti sonata. Dr. Hoffsteder and Miss Ellis, the president and director of the school, respectively, sat in back. Before the performance Freddie was so nervous he vomited, as all of us did. In the middle of the Scarlatti, Freddie suddenly lost his place and stopped. He got up, all 150 pounds of him, dressed in short pants and knee socks, and said, "Dr. Hoffsteder, Miss Ellis, may I begin again? I have a memory lapse." The second time Freddie stopped again at the same place. Again he rose, pleading, "Dr. Hoffsteder, Miss Ellis, may I begin again?" By this time the audience was in hysterics. I was laughing and his mother was crying. Freddie was determined not to stop a third time, and when he came to the passage he began improvising his way to the end. When he got his evaluation back it stated, "A very interesting interpretation . . ." Freddie had learned that you could snow the world if you did it with enough pizazz.

I was scared when the time came for my first Saturday morning concert, but my nervousness seemed to work for me. I liked the challenge, the electricity from the audience. The piece I played was one of my original compositions from Miss Shaeffer's Literature and Materials of Music class. There was much criticism from Edgar Roberts about the concert, but the audience's applause was tremendous. I saw then I was a performer.

Edgar was a fine teacher, but too rigid. He dissected the music too much, and we students just didn't have enough fun with the pieces. Juilliard in general was just too far removed from the real world. All we spoke about was what repertoire we were studying, and how many hours a day we practiced—I could manage four hours. The sun seemed to rise and set with Johann Sebastian Bach.

When I was nine, my Aunt Freda said, "Neil, it is high time for you to become a star. I've got an idea of how to get your career off the ground, but whatever you do, don't tell your mother. Eleanor feels you're much too young for auditions."

Aunt Freda had called the *Arthur Godfrey Talent Scouts* program. It was 1948 and the beginning of television's rise to pre-eminence, a time when the first TV stars were emerging. Every Christmas the Arthur Godfrey show held auditions for a children's television program. The audition that year brought almost 3,000 applicants, as well as their pushy show-business mothers and other screaming family members.

I made it through the early auditions with flying colors, and finally there were only five of us left, from which four would be chosen. For the final audition I played "Rustles of Spring" by Christian Sinding. I was so short that the producers in the booth had to stand to reassure themselves there was someone behind the music stand. I was very nervous, but when I had finished, I was sure I had won. Aunt Freda felt the same way, though the producers told us they would call us later with the final decision.

When we got home I burst in through the door and ran to tell Mom the news. Surprisingly, she was not upset about not being told beforehand—she was as excited as Aunt Freda and I. We sat by the phone all day waiting for the producers' call. My stomach was in knots.

"Sit down, Neil," Mom said. "You're not going to

make the phone ring any faster by wearing out the floor."

At last the call came through. After a tough decision, I had been disqualified. Mom and Aunt Freda were in tears. Although I was crushed, I was also secretly relieved. I had been scared to death that I would "freeze" on television.

Later, Aunt Freda tried to get me on *Ted Mack's Original Amateur Hour*. They were only interested, however, if I could play "Für Elise" with my elbows— that was the type of show it was. I was almost tempted to start practicing.

The two-bedroom apartment was beginning to empty out. Aunt May married Louie Borrocas. Aunt Kate married Jack Assael. Aunt Ann married her cousin, Charlie Benerdate. With some prodding by Mom, my grandmother and Aunt Molly moved into their own apartment a few blocks away, despite my father's protests. For the first time in my life, at age twelve, I had a normal-sized family.

My first performance as a singer occurred in my thirteenth year at my Bar Mitzvah.

I almost wasn't Bar Mitzvahed at all. Mother kept putting off Hebrew school for me. Between attending public school, Juilliard every Saturday, homework and piano practice, there was no time. But now that I was approaching thirteen, she thought something had to be done quickly. One cold October morning she escorted me to Temple Beth El in Manhattan Beach to enroll me.

The Bar Mitzvah, the Jewish ceremony at which a boy "becomes a man," consists of a morning religious service and, usually in the afternoon or evening, a party attended by family and friends. Through the years this party has become a Jewish superspectacle as each family tries to outdo the next. A great to-do is made over seating arrangements, table centerpieces, flowers, the orchestra, catering, the candle-lighting ceremony and picture taking. There is a Bar Mitzvah photo album to be savored by relatives for years to come. The hall sometimes has to be booked a full year in advance. Invitations are printed with RSVPs, and new clothes have to be bought. I have attended Bar Mitzvahs costing $50,000 and up.

As a taxi driver making $1,500 a year, my father, naturally, was frightened of the expense. He tried to discourage my mother, saying, "I'm short, Skinny," or, "What do you need it for?" or "In due time." Mother was not dissuaded—she was determined to have a Bar Mitzvah in the grand Jewish tradition, even if she had to go to work and pay for it herself. She found a job as a sales clerk at an A&S department store to finance my Bar Mitzvah.

Most Jewish boys start Hebrew school at the age of eight, or younger. When mother and I walked into the rabbi's private office at Beth El and introduced ourselves, I hadn't attended religious temple since I was a small child. Because we were not members of the Temple Beth El congregation, and as I was already twelve and a half, the rabbi flatly refused. "He's not properly prepared," the rabbi announced. "He has not received a formal Hebrew education."

The thought of her only son not being Bar Mitzvahed was unthinkable. "*Please*, Rabbi," Mother pleaded, tears welling up in her eyes. "How can you deny my boy his Bar Mitzvah? This is his heritage. How can I face my relatives?"

After fifteen minutes of my mother crying and beating her breast, he gave in, either from being convinced or to get rid of her.

"I'll make an exception this time," the rabbi said. "I'll accept him to Hebrew school, but he will have to work feverishly for the next six months toward his Bar Mitzvah."

I attended Hebrew school five days a week, from 3:30 to 5:00 P.M. after regular school. Soon I could read and write Hebrew so fluently I was able to teach my sister Ronnie as well. But the thing I enjoyed most was singing my Haftorah—the prayer that is sung in Hebrew at the Bar Mitzvah. I practiced every Saturday morning. One day I was rehearsing at Hebrew school and the cantor sat at the organ, smiling as he listened to me.

"Most of the boys can hardly carry a tune," he said. "Not only are you musical, but you have a remarkably beautiful, high alto voice." From then on, every Saturday the cantor would ask me to sing the Haftorah before the entire class.

March 13, the day of my Bar Mitzvah, finally arrived. When I got up that morning, my throat felt strange. After all the rehearsing, I had strained it. I was frightened. Playing the piano in front of an audience is one thing, but singing in public is a much bigger deal. Uncle Joey came to the house early to "lay *tfillin*" with me—saying a prayer while winding leather around your arm.

My family and I walked to Temple Beth El together. The temple was crowded, and I could see all my friends and relatives in the audience. There were two other boys who were also being Bar Mitzvahed. When the first two boys were finished, it was my turn to sing. I got up at the podium, and my stage fright vanished. By the end of the Haftorah there wasn't a dry eye in the house. I looked at the cantors. They flashed their congratulations. Mother beamed with pride, and everyone began hugging and kissing me. My voice, I had discovered, was an instrument with wide-ranging possibilities.

Afterwards the cantors took mother aside and suggested that she think seriously about her son becoming a cantor. She was flattered. "But I'm afraid Neil has other plans," she said. "He's getting a Ph.D. in music to be a teacher."

That night we had a marvelous party at Rosoff's restaurant in New York City—a night of music, food, candlelight and happiness. I received many fountain pens—the usual Bar Mitzvah gift. Cousin Robert, Aunt Minnie, Aunt Freda and Uncle Joey sang, and I played my perennial "Rustles of Spring." The evening was topped off by a Turkish dance performed by Norni and me. During the dance, the woman pastes a dollar bill on her forehead with spit and lures the man to her by shaking her shoulders and gyrating back and forth, ending up on the floor. The guests went wild.

Just before my Bar Mitzvah, Freddie moved to Bayside, Long Island. His parents had bought a house there for $12,000. They tried to convince us to buy a house as well, but father would not consider it.

"What do we need it for," he said. "It's only head-aches and mortgages. We don't make enough, Skinny. We're only paying $60 per month for this apartment."

My mother was despondent, but she could not per-suade him to take out a loan. So we stayed in Brighton Beach. I missed my friend; Bayside might as well have been the end of the world . . . different schools, a dif-ferent neighborhood. It was also quite a step up from Brighton.

By the time I entered P.S. 225 for the seventh and eighth grades, my classmates were asking me to play the piano at every opportunity. During assembly when the films broke down, and that was quite often, all the kids would start chanting, "We want Neil." As fright-ened as I was, I always got up and played. They seemed to love it, even though all I knew was classical. I was still very far from being a big shot. I was just a scrawny sissylike kid who happened to play the piano. I was not invited to parties, was not really accepted so-cially by the kids my age. I was a loner. "Maybe if I learned to play popular," I schemed, "I could gain their respect and not be such a social outcast."

I began to listen even more diligently to Martin Bloch's *Make Believe Ballroom*, which played such popular songs as "Mockingbird Hill," "Cry," "Tennes-see Waltz," "Truly Fair," and "Come On-a My House." My first attempts at pop chords were abomi-nable. But little by little, over several months, they im-proved. I often tried them out on Uncle Carl and Cousin Mona, occasionally accompanying myself with a vocal phrase or two, but very meekly. Uncle Carl said, "Your pop playing isn't great, but you have a nice voice."

During a family holiday at the Kenmore Lake Hotel in Livingston Manor, New York, that summer, Mrs. Greenfield, a neighbor who also lived at 3260 Coney Island Avenue in Brighton Beach, overheard me practicing the piano in the lobby.

"My son Howie, you know, is a poet," she said. "Perhaps you two could collaborate on a song."

I turned to her with a surprised look on my face. "I couldn't write a song," I told her. "I'm afraid I don't know how."

Nevertheless she had Howie ring our bell the following week back home. I could see right away that we weren't going to get along very well. He was sixteen, while I was only thirteen, and the age difference seemed to exacerbate our very different personalities. I tried to explain to him that I did not know how to write songs. Howie, however, convinced me to give it a try.

After several days I managed to finish my first song, "My Life's Devotion." "How did I do it?" I wondered to myself when I was finished. The notes and chords seemed to fall together. All I could think about as I wrote it was that I could play this for people and be somebody. The melody was a combination of a bastardized bolero in minor key, a ruptured rhumba, and probably some melodic fragment of a bad 1940s movie I had seen as a child. But I didn't care. It was a finished song.

We recorded it on Howie's recorder that evening. Howie's forgettable lyrics rhymed at the end of each line. My sister Ronnie thought it was awful, and she was right.

After "My Life's Devotion," I wrote a song a day for nearly twelve months. Neglecting my classical studies, I found that the tunes just seemed to flow out of me. Mother was angry because she felt I should be practicing concert repertory, but before long my songs were getting better, and even Mother had to agree that I showed talent.

One day my cousin Marleen Hoffman, one of the Brighton Thirteenth Street gang, heard me play my songs. As a result, miracle of miracles, I was invited to my first teenage party. Most of the popular kids in the neighborhood were attending, including "perfect" George Karp and Hank Medress, who became a member of the group I later founded, The Tokens. Everyone seemed to love my songs, and I really knew I had arrived when the girls turned their eyes from George Karp to listen to me for a few minutes.

CHAPTER 4

DOO-WOP

Then came rock 'n' roll.

With my new-found confidence, I started dating girls in 1952.

I was having pizza at Andrea's Pizza Parlor with Carol Klein, my girlfriend, who later became Carole King, creator of many rock classics.

There was a big flashing Wurlitzer jukebox at Andrea's, and out of it was blasting the strangest and most erotic sound I'd ever heard. It was called "Earth Angel," sung by The Penguins.

"It's got imperfections," I commented to Carole. We were pop music junkies and analyzed every hit record. "They're singing slightly off-key, but it's an honest reflection of the times we're living in, socially and emotionally, don't you think? Alan Freed calls it rock 'n' roll on his show."

"Whatever it is, it moves my ass," Carole said.

Carole was a scrawny girl with dirty blond hair, a long nose and funny buck teeth. She was one of a group of musical teenagers who hung around together singing on street corners and at sock hops.

Doo-wop singing originated in New York City. It was a spinoff from Black R & B records. The doo-wop group usually consisted of four or more singers. They would congregate on New York street corners, in schoolyards or in some hallway that had a natural echo. The songs they sang almost always had the same four chords, I, VI, II, V, or, in the key of C, C major, A minor, D minor, G major. The group sang a capella— without instrumentation. The lyrics dealt with young love, and the accents were unmistakably New York.

Carole and I would jump up and dance when Alan Freed played doo-wop on WINS: "Why Do Fools Fall in Love?" by Frankie Lymon and The Teenagers, "Sh-Boom" by The Chords and by The Crewcuts, "Earth Angel" of course, "The Closer You Are" by the Chanels, "Life Is But a Dream" by The Harp Tones, "Over the Mountain" by Johnny and Joe, "Eddie My Love" by The Teen Queens, "In the Still of the Night" by The Five Satins, and The Elegants' "Little Star."

The bass singers usually had an intricate part, jumping up and down octaves. There was always a high falsetto on top. The harmonies were close, in triad style. There were lots of shoo-bops, sha-la-las, lang-a-langs, shoo-doops and shoo-be-doos.

Carole and I swooned over them. We did a kind of

bump-and-grind slow dance to them called The Fish. It gave Carole and me a chance to get *very* close to each other. Bodies rubbed. It got sexy and sensuous.

Alan Freed also played rhythm and blues records, which were then impossible to buy in regular record stores. Carole King and I searched out the original black recordings in ghetto stores. From these records by black artists, singers like Pat Boone, who did Little Richard's "Tutti-Frutti," and Georgia Gibbs, who did Lavern Baker's black version of "Tweedle Dee," would record arrangements for the traditionally white audience. *Billboard* magazine once listed both versions of "Tweedle Dee," Lavern Baker's and Georgia Gibbs's.

Howie Greenfield had not heard rock 'n' roll before. When I played some songs for him he thought it was a passing fad. I think the reason he felt that way was that he couldn't write rock 'n' roll lyrics easily. His hero had always been the lyricist Lorenz Hart. A far cry from "Earth Angel." Finally I convinced him to give it a try, and we sat down and wrote our first rock 'n' roll song, "Mr. Moon."

I tried it out on the Brighton Thirteenth Street gang, with whom I had become friends. They loved it. In the tryouts for the annual talent "Bally-hoo" that year at Abraham Lincoln High School, I sang "Mr. Moon" with a drum and saxophone backup. I made it.

This was a tough school, with fifty percent of the kids from the ghetto neighborhood of Coney Island. On the day of the "Bally-hoo," I played the first of two scheduled performances and was amazed to see the effect my "Mr. Moon" had on the kids. As I finished the crowd went wild—the students exploded into something resembling a large-scale riot. The toughs in their leather jackets and duck's ass haircuts started trashing the auditorium. Absolute pandemonium. I felt a perverse rush, as if someone had shot me up with a drug. For a few moments the sissy was a hero.

The principal and teachers were naturally horrified. Immediately following the show I was called to the principal's office.

"Neil, you're a fine classical pianist," Mr. Lass, the principal said, "but that rock 'n' roll has got to go. I'm afraid that I must request that you omit 'Mr. Moon' from the second performance and play something less wild."

Word, however, had gotten around, and in the space of a few hours a petition was circulated and signed by several hundred kids demanding "Mr. Moon" be repeated.

In the auditorium, when it was my turn to go on, the students began to stand and clap and stomp their feet. "We want 'Mr. Moon,' we want Neil; we want 'Mr. Moon,' we want Neil." At last the principal gave in, and once again the walls reverberated with rock 'n' roll.

Suddenly I was a high school celebrity. Music, I discovered, was my ticket to popularity. Everyone who had put me down, ignored me or made fun of me, began to make friends. I was welcomed into the backroom of the Sweet Shop, the local hangout where Alfred Avazzo and "Frenchie," the school bigshots, held court—kids in dungarees and black leather sneaking illicit cigarettes, listening to the sounds of Fats Domino and Chuck Berry on the jukebox. My classical training began to take a back seat in my musical affections.

In my first year at Lincoln High School, 1953, I played in Ben Goldman's band class, as well as being the pianist for Mrs. Eisen's choral group and playing for various senior shows directed by Ed and Hazel Shapiro. One day Bill Medine, a teacher at Lincoln High, heard me playing in the auditorium with the dance band. He was so impressed he asked me to meet with him.

"Neil, have you ever thought of a music counselor's job at a summer camp?"

I was really caught off-guard. Camp was for rich kids. I had only heard stories about how much fun it was.

Mr. Medine went on, "I'm the owner of Camp Echo Lake, in Lake George, New York. I'd like to offer you a job as music counselor for the summer. We could really use someone with your talent. The pay isn't great, but you'd have free use of all the recreational facilities there, and all the food you can eat."

I couldn't believe it—going to camp for free and being paid at the same time. I told him I would love to, but that I'd have to talk it over with my mother. Mom and I discussed it that evening, and she agreed that it would be a marvelous opportunity. The next day I gave Bill Medine my answer. At thirteen and a half, I was about to become music counselor at Camp Echo Lake.

That summer all the mothers and their kids congregated at Grand Central Station to say goodbye. This was my first time away from home, and when it came

time to board the train, tears sprang to my eyes. My
mother tried to hold back her tears, but it was useless.
We hugged one last time, and the next thing I knew I
was looking out the window of the train, waving goodbye. Not wanting to be too conspicuous, I wiped my
face and sat very bravely for the rest of the trip.

Bill, as Mr. Medine asked me to call him, put me in
bunk "O" with the fifteen-year-olds. Bunking with
them was an eye opener for a Jewish mama's boy. The
boys were all good ballplayers and seasoned campers.
They thought nothing of cursing or fighting at the drop
of a hat. They looked at me, a soft-spoken, high-voiced
kid, as something of a freak. I was four-and-a-half feet
tall, painfully thin, with thick glasses, braces on my
teeth and I looked like Crusader Rabbit. "Are you from
England?" they kept asking me, upon hearing me
speak. Most of them used slang and weren't used to
hearing someone speak properly and articulately. I un-
packed my trunk very neatly and sat by myself, terrified that one of them would punch me out if I looked at
him the wrong way.

The counselor for bunk O was named Bogie. He was
an athletic, red-headed guy, a real jock, who always had
the best ballplayers in his bunk. He couldn't seem to
understand how he had gotten me. He must have decided right away that he didn't like me, because I could
tell he was out to get me. That night I listened to the
foulest language I had ever heard. I tried to stay out of
everyone's way as much as I could. The bunk was small
and I didn't get much sleep.

The next morning, the bugle sounded at eight, and
everyone lined up around the flagpole, girls on one side,

boys on the other. The air was crisp and clean, the pine trees beautiful. Once again I felt glad to be there.

After breakfast a beautiful woman in her thirties named Mollie Gordon introduced herself to me.

"Aren't you the new music counselor?" she asked. Mollie was the dramatic counselor. She seemed surprised that I was so young, but soon we were off on a discussion of the camp's musical schedule for the summer. "Each age group puts on one musical during the summer, so that will mean four musicals altogether," she explained. "Unfortunately, since the camp can't afford to buy the music rights to the musicals, we don't have any music scores. Part of your job is to listen to the original sound tracks on the record player and pick up the music off the records by ear in order to teach the songs to the kids."

I swallowed nervously, though in fact I should have had no reason to be wary—after all the years of picking up songs from the radio, I had a very good ear for popular music and musical comedy. I could transpose easily—it was work that I loved.

Mollie smiled at me, a big country-girl grin that made me feel confident and relaxed, saying, "I'm sure you'll be wonderful."

I decided then that regardless of Bogie and the others of bunk O, I was going to have a terrific summer.

The camp would not allow any calls from parents for the first week. When my mother finally got through, we shed a few tears on the phone. I told her I missed her terribly, but that I thought I was going to like camp a lot.

One morning shortly afterwards, during breakfast,

Bogie heard me complain that my portion of scrambled eggs was too small. He was in a bitchy mood.

"Give me an order of fifteen eggs," he demanded. When a plate loaded with eggs was handed to him, he shoved them in front of me. "You want eggs—here's eggs. And you're going to eat them. Every one of them. Or so help me I'll cram them down your throat."

With Bogie standing over me I somehow managed to get them all down, but it was a terrible thing to do. Immediately afterwards I became very sick, and had to drag myself to the camp infirmary. When Bogie heard, however, he came running after me and yanked me out by the neck before the doctor could get to me.

"You're going to make your bed first. I'll be damned if I'm going to let you loaf in a hospital bed all day because of a few eggs. And after you make your bunk you're going to clean the cabin."

I replied by throwing up all over him. Despite my stomachache, this small revenge made me feel better.

One of the good things I discovered that summer at camp, however, was love. I had noticed a really cute-looking girl at the table in front of me at mealtimes, and one day I introduced myself.

"My name is Ellen," she said. "Ellen Berland."

I fell in love with her immediately. Fortunately she was interested in music, and we had long conversations after dinner, sitting by the lake as the evening turned to night. One night, in desperation, I put my arm around her and kissed her. I felt a wonderful burning sensation in the pit of my stomach. She didn't resist—in fact she shyly kissed me back. From that moment on we went everywhere together.

Once the camp began rehearsing for the musicals my popularity grew immensely. Mollie was delightful to work with—a complete professional. That summer we put on *The Mikado*, *Peter Pan*, *Pajama Game*, and *Annie Get Your Gun*, and with each musical my popularity increased. Even the guys in bunk O started to come around (after, that is, short-sheeting my bed a few times and putting various animals in it). By the end of the summer I had written a number of original camp songs; some, such as "Swift as the Wind" and "On to the Fray" are still sung today. Bill Medine was very pleased with my work, and at the end of the summer he proudly handed me a check for $25. Technically, I was a professional.

CHAPTER 5
THE TOKENS

My freshman year I toyed around with the idea of forming my own singing group, but it never got off the ground. I continued to practice classical and popular piano at home and write songs with Howie. One day in math class about a year after the "Bally-hoo" show I overheard a kid named Jay Siegel softly singing falsetto in the seat next to me. His voice was pure, high and utterly captivating. As we left class after the bell I asked him, out of the blue, "Would you be interested in joining a vocal group I'm starting?" I had always loved records with vocal harmonies and "part" singing, especially rock 'n' roll records of the doo-wop school.

"Sure," he said. "What kind of music?"

"Doo-wop."

I asked three fellow singers from Mrs. Eisen's choral

class, Cynthia Zolotin, Eddie Rapkin, and Hank Medress, to join my doo-wop group, and The Tokens were formed. It was soon apparent that we got along very well together. We rehearsed every day and I instructed them in harmony, part singing, breathing and intonation. The Tokens were an extension of my creative writing, a chance to work up what I composed. The group was also a great source of income, singing at sock hops, Bar Mitzvahs and weddings. I was already making some money as a piano teacher with eight or nine students.

Cynthia Zolotin's mother knew a man by the name of Happy Goday, a music publisher who had "connections in the biz." She set up an appointment for The Tokens to audition for him. This was our chance to really make something of ourselves as a group.

Happy Goday had offices in the Brill Building at 1619 Broadway, the heart of Tin Pan Alley, headquarters for the songwriters and music publishers of America.

On the appointed day we arrived early. Happy escorted us into his office and had us audition right there. At Happy's request we sang three songs, and awaited his verdict with bated breath.

"I like you," he said at last. "I think you've got commercial possibilities. But there's something wrong with your singing," he went on, pointing at me. "You don't pronounce your Ts and Ds right."

Nevertheless, Happy signed us up to a short-term contract and arranged an audition with Morty Kraft, a record producer and owner of an independent record label called Melba Records. Melba already had two national hits to its credit, "Alone" by The Sheppard Sisters and "Church Bells May Ring" by The Willows. Morty Kraft was a record mogul who seemed to ooze power and money. He arranged a recording session for us to do four of the songs Howie and I had written: "I Love My Baby," "While I Dream," "Don't Go," and "Come Back, Joe."

We rehearsed furiously for days, struggling to get everything just right. On the day of the recording session we filed nervously into the dark, menacing-looking studio in the basement of a building on the west side of Manhattan. We could smell marijuana smoke coming from the next room, and the stench of whiskey filled the air. It was seedy and depressing. Four shaking teenagers from Brooklyn . . . our first time ever in a recording studio. We knew this was our big chance.

"You only have two hours to record all four songs. Make sure you do the things right the first time," we were advised.

Immediately the group started to fall apart. Eddie began singing flatter and flatter, and Hank and Cynthia seemed to be in shock. We huddled around that menacing microphone, holding on to each other for dear life. We had practiced for months and this was it. We knew it. The backup band to our vocals was made up of five black musicians hired by the studio who had never seen the music before. Each wrong chord they played was like a knife going through my insides. I remember hearing the words, "Take 20 . . . take 21 . . ." It was torture. I realized later that we should have rehearsed with these musicians a few times before recording. The tempo got faster and faster. Our vocals grew more hectic with each take. "I Love My Baby" sounded like four frightened chipmunks, each fighting to be heard above the others.

"Listen guys, we've got to relax," I told the others. Somehow I was able to put the others at ease, cracking jokes, coaxing us back into sync. Finally the record started to take shape, and miraculously, we finished the session.

"I Love My Baby" was released shortly afterward, and as a result Ted Steele, the host of the teenage New York television show, had us on the air. (Ted was Alison Steele's husband and Alison later became "The Nightbird" on WNEW-FM.) A month later, while listening to Peter Trippe's Top 40 "Hits of the Week," I heard him say, "We're very proud of our local group, The Tokens, with our number 32 song this week, 'I Love My Baby.'" I went crazy and called everyone immediately. Happy Goday, our publisher, was counting his money already.

Our fame, however, was short-lived. The record fizzled out and became only a local New York phenomenon, climbing as high as the twenties on the New York charts.

There was another song of mine receiving air time. My sister Ronnie had recently married Edward Grossman, a Ph.D. in chemistry whom she had dated for many months. Ed liked to play guitar and write songs in his spare time. One day, while the three of us were sitting around in Ed's dorm at Columbia University, Ed and I wrote a song called "Never Again." He took it to a publishing house and placed it with the great singer Dinah Washington. Her recording became a national R & B hit, and also made Peter Trippe's WMGM Top 40. At the age of fifteen I had two songs on that Top 40 at the same time. I was gaining a reputation in New York music circles.

CHAPTER 6
CAROLE KING

My old girlfriend Carole King came back into my life. At school one day she said, "Would you mind if some friends and I came over to hear you rehearse sometime?"

"No, not at all," I replied. We often had friends drop by. "Why don't you come tonight?"

That evening, with an audience of five new faces, we played our hearts out. I loved to perform. When I took a break at the piano, Carole sat down and tried to emulate me, crudely playing my songs with one finger. She had perfect pitch and could harmonize at the drop of a hat.

Carole began coming to every rehearsal, and we began to play musical games together. "Carole," I would ask, "tell me what notes I'm playing." I would press down several keys with both hands. "You have to tell me every note without looking at the piano."

Carole would pick out the notes flawlessly. "You're playing F, A flat, A, B flat, B, C, E, and G with the right hand and two perfect fifths, C and G and G and D, with your left." Everyone in the room would gasp and applaud.

Soon Carole and I were dating again. I think what I was attracted to most was her extraordinary love for music. One night at a dance in Brighton, I turned to her and said, "Do you want to have some fun? I'm tired of this music. Let's sit at the piano and sing some doo-wop songs." Within minutes the piano was surrounded by kids listening to our harmonies.

Soon Carole and I could re-create every piano fill or musical lick on the original rock 'n' roll recordings. We listened to the radio religiously and knew every song in the Top 40. Within a short while, Carole and I began to attract our own following. When the word got out we were attending a dance, fans chased after us, hoping to see us perform. We were high school celebrities.

Carole's mother couldn't stand me. Carole was a straight-A student, and her mother felt I was a bad influence on her daughter. Carole started a group called The Cosigns because of me, and we seemed to go everywhere together. One Sunday shortly after we'd started going steady, I asked Carole if she'd like to go mambo dancing in Lakewood, New Jersey. Her mother almost said no. But when I informed Mrs. Klein that my mother and father would be driving and chaperoning, Carole was given permission to go. We picked her up at her family's apartment on Ocean Avenue and

Avenue Z in a borrowed car, as we didn't own one. My mother whispered to me as Carole got in, "Couldn't you pick a pretty one?" I whispered back, "Wait till you hear her sing and play the piano. Then tell me what you think."

It was a three-hour drive from Brighton to Lakewood, and Carole and I had the radio constantly blaring rock 'n' roll songs as we sat in the back of the car holding hands and singing lyrics. Our relationship was already much more than just musical—for the second time in my life I was in love.

At age sixteen, Carole was already a heavy smoker. During the car ride she constantly lit one cigarette after another. My mother was horrified. Nice girls, she felt, didn't smoke. When we got to the hotel, she took me aside.

"Why does she smoke like that? What do you see in her?"

"Mother leave her alone. She's amazing, and incredibly talented."

Carole and I spent a wonderful day dancing to the mambo band. During the dance breaks we each took turns entertaining the hotel guests at the piano to their appreciative applause.

By evening I wanted desperately to be alone with her. More than anything else in the world I wanted to touch her, to have her in my arms and kiss her.

Later as we returned to Brooklyn, Carole and I sat in the back seat kissing and petting.

The Tokens were in trouble. The problem arose when Alan Freed, on his radio show, did not play the A

side of our record, "I Love My Baby," but the B side,
"While I Dream," which I sang solo. It started to get a
lot of attention, which caused dissension within the
group. There was a fight over who was to sing lead
vocals.

I had a crush on Cynthia Zolotin and was giving her
leads in many of the songs we were doing. Eddie Rapkin took offense over the lead vocals I was giving her,
and I left the group. After my departure The Tokens
reorganized with Hank and Jay remaining and the
Margo brothers being added. They scored a smash hit
with "The Lion Sleeps Tonight."

Carole King was always around, too. She'd be wher-
ever the Tokens and I sang. We'd dated off and on for
three years. She followed me around. She copied me;
she worshiped me. Her mother still disapproved of me,
but I told Mrs. Klein that Carole would be famous
someday. Carole was a pushy little kid. She always
showed up at my record sessions. She was a groupie, a
Neil Sedaka groupie. And she would always slip herself into the photographs somehow.

CHAPTER 7
DON KIRSHNER

In 1956, while I was a senior in high school, Mr. Goldman, the music teacher at Lincoln, suggested that I try out for the WQXR piano competition. This was a citywide classical competition, and five winners were chosen each year from New York high schools to play a live broadcast on the radio. The first audition was at radio station WQXR, the classical music station of *The New York Times*. Abram Chasens was in charge. I played a prelude and fugue from Bach's *The Well-Tempered Clavier*, *Reflet Dans L'Eau* by Debussy, the Prokofiev *Third Piano Sonata*, and the G-minor *Ballade* of Chopin. I passed the preliminary auditions with little difficulty.

The final audition was attended and judged by the

great Artur Rubinstein. He liked my playing immensely; I could see his face beaming as I played. In fact, on his report, he commented, "Mr. Sedaka, I especially liked the G-minor *Ballade*."

I was in seventh heaven. I waited impatiently over the next few days for the results, which were being sent by mail. At last they arrived. I had won.

Lincoln High School was in an uproar. My family and friends bought their tickets way in advance and during the broadcast sat first row. WQXR had a studio with several hundred seats. As I walked out onstage upon hearing my name called, I panicked—the thought of having to play those difficult pieces on the radio scared me to death. Somehow, miraculously, I got through them, though I think I did it on automatic pilot. The audience's applause made it all worthwhile.

On Saturday, however, Edgar Roberts, my piano teacher, was not so pleased. He had recorded the concert on a wire recorder, and he found a lot of faults in my performance. "The Prokofiev had no dynamics—it was all double forte. *Reflet Dans L'Eau* was rushed. And you didn't play the Bach with the proper subtleties."

My triumph turned into disaster. At that time whatever Edgar Roberts said was gospel.

I was somewhat discouraged with classical music for many reasons. Most important was that it had a limited public and there was not a great deal of money in it. I had tasted success as a songwriter and had already been on in front of audiences and on radio with The Tokens and liked the notorietyand recognition. And rock 'n' roll was flourishing. Still, when I graduated from Lincoln

High School in 1956, I was persuaded to enter the Juilliard School.

The piano teacher that I wanted at Juilliard was Rosina Lhévinne, whose fame was legendary. Edgar Roberts told me disparagingly, "Don't even bother, you're not dedicated enough." The other great teacher at Juilliard was Adele Marcus. I auditioned for her at her apartment on West Fifty-seventh Street, and she was so impressed that she immediately took me on as one of her students. She was more fun than Edgar, and I found myself actually enjoying the sessions.

Nevertheless, as Edgar Roberts had predicted, I started to neglect my practice of classical music. I found it taking second seat to songwriting with Howie Greenfield. I was now placing my songs with many recording artists, and later had several R & B hits, including "Since You've Been Gone" by Clyde McPhatter, "I Waited Too Long" by Lavern Baker, and "Bring Me Love" by The Clovers.

Then Howie and I stumbled across a new publishing firm at 1650 Broadway owned by Al Nevins and Don Kirshner called Aldon Music. Al Nevins had been a member of an instrumental group called The Three Sons, a very successful group on RCA Records. Don Kirshner, his partner, just out of high school, was a friend of Bobby Darin, who was about to become a major rock 'n' roll star.

Howie and I had just auditioned a new song called "Stupid Cupid" for the president of Hill and Range, which was turned down. Walking out of the office we ran into the great songwriters Pomus and Schuman, who said, "Oh, by the way, on the fourth floor there's a new music firm opening up, Aldon Music. Why don't you take your songs there? They're looking for new writers."

Howie and I ran for the stairs and sprinted to the fourth floor. When Don Kirshner answered the door, I said, "We're songwriters and we'd like to play some new material."

Don Kirshner did not look impressed. "I'm awfully sorry, we're in conference at the moment," he said. If there was any such conference, it must have been to figure out how they would pay their first month's rent. Don Kirshner was sweeping the floor—they had only opened one week before and were still setting up shop. "Come back in two hours," he told us.

We went back to Nevins and Kirshner two hours later and played them ten songs, including "Stupid Cupid." They were overwhelmed.

"Did you really write them yourselves?" Kirshner asked.

"Yes," I assured them, "we're the writers."

We must have made a strange-looking team. I was still about four-and-a-half feet tall; Howie was six feet. We looked like Mutt and Jeff. Don Kirshner became very excited—he saw potential and made no effort to hide his enthusiasm. Nevins, a man with a very cool, suave, European personality, was more reserved. He told us to come back the next day to discuss contracts. Our eyes lit up—here was our big chance.

The next day Nevins signed Howie and me to exclusive songwriting contracts, as well as signing me to a manager-artist contract.

In the summer of 1957, I became the house pianist at the Lake Tarelton Club in Pike, New Hampshire, a luxurious resort owned by the Jacobs family, famous for their Festival of the Seven Arts. I was hired by Hal Graham, the orchestra leader, and at eighteen I was the youngest by far of the eight members. It was a marvelous summer, for I not only had a chance to play dance music, but also to accompany such great artists as Norman Scott and Regina Resnik from the Metropolitan Opera. Manny Sacks, the president of RCA, gave lectures, along with many other notables from show business. The "Incomparable" Hildegarde's manager, Miss Anna Sosenko, was there that summer, and hearing me play songs in the lobby, she introduced herself. She was a very notorious character in the business. Tapping her hand on the piano she made one comment to me that I will never forget. "Always sing your own compositions, my boy."

While at the hotel I met a comedian named Lenny Maxwell, who liked what he heard of me. At the end of the summer, Lenny took me to meet his friend Phil Ramone, a recording engineer. Phil later became a great record producer for Billy Joel and Paul Simon. He had some sophisticated equipment in his apartment, and he helped me make a piano and voice demo of two of my songs, "Laura Lee" and "Snowtime." Lenny Maxwell took the tapes home with him. Several months later, he rang our bell at 3260 Coney Island Avenue and surprised me with a finished master on Decca Records. I was thrilled—it was the first time my voice had been on a record as a soloist.

"Let's take it to the local radio stations to see if we can promote it," Lenny said.

After much calling we managed to get me booked on a television show in New Haven, Connecticut. The artist before me was a beautiful, shy-looking, nine-year-old child with the most extraordinary voice I had ever heard—Brenda Lee, a name the recording industry was to hear much of in the coming years. At last it was my turn, and to the voice-over of my record I lip-synched "Laura Lee" and "Snowtime." The applause was minimal.

After the show we drove back to Brooklyn, and the whole way back I prayed for a snowstorm, anything to help "Snowtime." My prayers were partially answered—we had one of the biggest snowstorms in years. Unfortunately it didn't help. "Snowtime" was snowbound—it received almost no air time.

I was to have better luck with "Stupid Cupid" and a young lady who came into my life at this time named Connie Francis.

CHAPTER 8
CONNIE FRANCIS

One of Don Kirshner's best friends, Connie Francis, was the number one female vocalist in the country in 1958, riding the top spot on the charts with the song "Who's Sorry Now?" One day Donnie called Howie and me into his office and announced, "I was with Connie Francis last night and I'm convinced I've talked her into recording one of your songs." He made arrangements for us to get together, and the next week Kirshner, Howie and I agreed to meet Connie Francis in Newark, where she was having her hair done. We circled around the block for almost three hours before La Prima Donna came out. If you didn't know she was the number one female vocalist before meeting her, you knew it when she stepped into that car. She handled herself like a superstar—every gesture and expression

full of self-confidence. She let us know she was somebody.

I was very nervous, sitting there next to *the* Connie
Francis. My palms were sweaty and I kept nervously
rubbing them on my pants. We drove about forty-five
minutes to her home in Nutley, New Jersey, the long-
est forty-five minutes of my life. Fortunately the conversation was no problem—Howie and I listened while
she talked.

Her entire family was there when we arrived. Sitting
down at her piano I began to play what I thought was
our best ballad. Connie Francis was not impressed. I
tried a second ballad, and she politely said, "Very
nice." As I attempted a third, she started to dial the
phone. I was losing her. Turning to Howie I said, "I'm
going to play 'Stupid Cupid' for her." Howie immediately motioned Don Kirshner to a pow-wow.

"You can't play 'Stupid Cupid,' " Howie said. "You
promised it to The Sheppard Sisters. They're recording it in a week or two."

"I don't care," I replied. "I'm here with Connie
Francis, the number one singer in the country. She
hasn't liked any of our ballads. I'm going to play a rock
'n' roll song."

I played "Stupid Cupid" and when I finished Connie
Francis jumped to her feet, saying "That's my next
record. I'm going to make that my next hit." She said
she liked it all the more because it was in the style of
her favorite female singer, Jo Ann Campbell.

Connie Francis recorded "Stupid Cupid" for MGM
Records. The producer was Morty Kraft, and he and
Connie Francis both asked me to be the pianist on the

session. There were several glissandos in the score, where I had to take my thumb and run it down the keyboard. I was so hyped up that I tore open the skin of my thumb and bled all over the piano, but I refused to stop playing.

By the end of the session I knew we had a hit. The record came out in 1958, and it became an international smash, reaching number one in most countries, and as high as number seventeen on the official U.S. *Billboard* chart. When our first royalty check came in the mail I was astonished—it was for $8,000, the largest check I'd seen in my life. I handed it over to my mother, and she showed it to all her friends. Everyone was amazed that we could make that much money from writing a song. Suddenly songwriting became quite respectable. "Stupid Cupid" brought in about $20,000 that year between record sales, sheet music, radio and TV. Howie and I were now a professional team.

Somehow Harry Finfer, a Philadelphia-based producer, got his hands on a demo of me singing a song I had written called "Ring a Rockin' Music"—a song that was not one of my big efforts. I found out about it one evening when I turned on Dick Clark's rock 'n' roll program, *American Bandstand*. I almost fell out of my chair when Dick Clark announced—"And now here's a new singer, Neil Sedaka, with his song 'Ring a Rockin' Music.' " I stared at the screen in disbelief. Screaming to my mother, "They're using my song on the Dick Clark show," I called her to the TV set. We both looked on in shock as the regulars danced to it.

The record did not become a success. But Al Nevins, being a smart businessman, contacted the show and told Dick Clark's staff to keep an eye out for forthcoming records from me. Although "Ring a Rockin' Music" didn't sell much, at least Clark's airing showed there was interest in my kind of singing.

In the summer of 1958 I formed a band called The Nordanels with Norman Spizz, a trumpeter, and David Bass, a drummer. Later we added Howard Tischler on sax. Norman and Dave tried to talk me out of going back to the Lake Tarelton Club, and instead going to the swinging Catskill Mountains. "At some of these resorts up there we can get laid every night," Norman told me. Norman knew of a place in Monticello, New York, called the Esther Manor Hotel. "I'm this close to Sam Graham, the agent," he said, holding his fingers together. "And Sam Graham can get us the gig for the whole summer."

I was persuaded. "Okay. I'll tell the Lake Tarelton Club I'm not coming."

The three of us arrived at the Esther Manor Hotel just a few days previous to the summer season, and a tall blond woman walked out of the dining room to greet us.

"I'm awfully sorry, boys," she said, "but all the waiter and busboy jobs have been filled."

"Esther Strassberg?" Norman asked. "Let me introduce myself. I am Norman Spizz, and we are The Nordanels—your new band for the summer."

All Esther Strassberg saw was three teenagers, boys really, standing in the lobby of a plush resort, claiming to be the hotel's summer band. She screamed, "Get me Sam Graham on the phone. Is he trying to ruin me?"

"Please," Norman pleaded with her. "At least give us a chance. We're really very good. Neil here not only sings and plays the piano, but writes his own songs too."

Esther reluctantly agreed to let us play at a private party at the hotel before the season opened. To her amazement and delight, people liked us. Everyone seemed to be dancing. We sang some of the standard hits as well as our own songs, including "Stupid Cupid," which was a big hit. Norman was charming and seemed to know his way around the older women, keeping them happy.

Whatever the guests liked, Esther liked. We got the job for the summer.

That summer was special for another reason besides music. On entering the lobby the next day, I saw a beautiful girl behind the reception desk. I stopped dead in my tracks. She had large expressive eyes, a sensual smile and a warm, winning face. I immediately fell in love with her. Turning to Norman I said, "You see that girl at the desk? I'm going to marry her."

Norman was used to my impulsiveness. "Are you nuts, Neil. She's only sixteen years old. She's a baby." Summoning up my courage, I walked over to the desk.

"Hi," I said, looking into those beautiful eyes. "I'm Neil Sedaka, part of The Nordanels. Are you working here for the summer?"

"I'm Esther's daughter, Leba," she said.

When I told her I was a songwriter, she didn't believe me. "What have you written?" she asked.

"I have a song called 'Stupid Cupid' sung by Connie Francis that's just come out."

"Connie Francis? Sure," she smirked.

The next night she heard the song on the radio and realized I was telling the truth. From that moment on we began to go out together, and by the end of the summer I was truly in love.

Back in Manhattan I was still clinging to classical music, but I began skipping class. I'd take the train to the Apollo Theatre in Harlem to hear singers like Ray Charles. One day Adele, my piano teacher, said to me after my lesson, "I hear you have a hit on your hands."

"Yes," I said, a little embarrassed.

"Don't be embarrassed," she said. "It's a very well-crafted song. I knew I was going to lose you to the pop world. But I will give you a word of advice. For your own sake, never stop playing classical music. Always have a Beethoven sonata under your fingers, or a Chopin étude. It will always be an asset."

It was some of the best advice I have ever had.

My keyboard harmony teacher at Juilliard, Frances Goldstein (she had busted Fred Gershon's chops for years as his piano teacher), had insisted when I entered the college level at Juilliard that I be put in Keyboard Harmony II, second-year-level keyboard. Despite my protests she felt I could handle it. The course consisted of reading difficult orchestral scores at the keyboard from sight, scores that included at least twelve staffs with parts for oboe, flutes, clarinet and strings. Some of the parts were written in the alto clef. Frances was tough, and when I couldn't handle it, she flunked me.

I decided that was the last straw. I burned all my scores and I decided to take a leave of absence from

Juilliard for six months. My mother told me, "If nothing happens with your pop music in six months, you must return to school."

My sister thought I was making a big mistake. "There are thousands of people who can sing and write songs, but very few who are good enough to be classical pianists." Nevertheless, I was ready to give songwriting my all.

"Stupid Cupid" reached number 16 in *Cash Box*, and had edged out "Volare" from the top spot in England. I let Nevins and Kirshner know that now that I was a full-fledged songwriter with a hit record under my belt, my dream was to record my own songs.

Al Nevins wanted me to audition for RCA, but he wanted me to wait for the right song. Being very impatient, I kept pushing him. But Al's sense of timing was impeccable, and he convinced me that we had to wait. Finally, the right song did come along, "The Diary," which Howie and I had written for Little Anthony and The Imperials as a follow-up to their smash, "Tears On My Pillow." But unfortunately they ruined the song, changing the words and altering melodies. Al and I looked at each other and shook our heads. Al Nevins said, "Why not make 'The Diary' your first recording on RCA Victor?"

When I played "The Diary" on the piano for Fred Gershon, his reaction was negative. "Neil, you can't record that song. It sounds like 'Diarrheeee-a.'"

Nevertheless, the following week Al brought me to the office of Steve Sholes to audition. Steve was head of A & R, Artists and Repertoire, at RCA, and was responsible for signing up new talent. A couple of years before, he had signed up Elvis Presley from Sun Records. He was huge—at least 300 pounds—but very amiable, and he had a clear sense of what the record-buying public wanted. He immediately put me at ease.

Al had been talking me up over the past several weeks, so by the time I sat down and sang "The Diary" on his small upright piano, it was virtually already sold. RCA realized from the Presley phenomenon that there were a lot of teenage record buyers out there. Before, they had concentrated primarily on classical and very polished pop recordings. The thought of another Elvis Presley excited them.

Steve Sholes immediately made plans for a recording session at RCA's East Twenty-fourth Street studio. A few days later I signed a contract. Because I was young and green and had no legal advice, my mother and I really had no idea what we were signing. After years of waiting for such an opportunity, I only cared that I was recording on a major label. I was blind to anything else. I found out later that Nevins and Kirshner received several thousand dollars advance—while I got none at all.

Al set up the sessions and hired the musicians and singers. On the day of the session, he sat at the control board. My demonstration record was used to familiarize the other musicians. There were at least fifteen musicians and five singers, what we called "readers"—proficient vocalists who could sight sing. Their pitch was good, too good as it turned out.

The session started out well, but after a couple of hours, I knew the magic was missing. The record sounded too legitimate—slick and polished. It just

didn't sound like rock 'n' roll. Al, in his cool and consoling fashion, said, "Neil, don't worry." We sat down
and discussed how "The Diary" could be salvaged.

"Why don't we try it again with a small rhythm section," I said, "a few friends of mine can sing background."

"I think you're right," Al replied, and we both
agreed to re-back the session.

I called Armand Sorrentino, Howard Tischler, and
Bert Dashóe, all close friends, for back-up vocals, and
the four of us re-recorded "The Diary" the next week.
At last it sounded right. The less sophisticated voices of
my friends made the difference. This second recording
of "The Diary" sounded more like the hits on the top of
the *Billboard* charts.

RCA agreed. So much so they were willing to put
$100,000 behind promoting "The Diary." They hired
independent promotion men and gave television sets to
the radio stations to give out as gifts. DJs ran "Diary"
contests on the air in return for airline tickets to exotic
places. It was a legal form of payola. *Time* magazine, in
fact, did a small story on RCA's ad campaign for "The
Diary." RCA even printed up single sheet diaries and
for the first time in history, a singer's photo was put on
the label of the DJs' promotional copies.

I took to the road with Don Kirshner to visit radio
stations. The fast-talking DJs seemed a little leery of
this skinny new singer with a high voice whose name
they could hardly pronounce.

While we were in Pittsburgh a call came in from Ira
Howard, Leba Strassberg's first cousin and the editor
of *Cashbox* magazine. It was the dead of winter, and we

had five hops to do that night, all in and around Pittsburgh. Hops were teenage dances where the artist would come to lip-synch to his record. I was in the lobby of the hotel when Donnie returned from the phone.

"Sit down, Neil," he said. "Ira Howard just called. Hold on to your seat. 'The Diary' has just entered the Top 100 like a bullet at number 62."

I was speechless. I felt as if someone had handed me $10 million. After six years of writing songs and knocking on doors, being turned down by record companies and feeling discouraged, I had made the charts as a recording star. I broke down in tears. Nineteen years old and number 62 on the charts. I thought, what else is there in life?

We continued on to Cleveland and Chicago, and "The Diary" was beginning to play on every station.

Not all was to be peaches and cream, however. When we arrived in Chicago, I was scheduled to do the Marty Faye radio and TV shows. He had a local interview program and was noted for controversial and sarcastic remarks, especially about new rock 'n' roll singers. That was his big draw. The radio show was scheduled for the afternoon. It was my first radio interview. Marty played my recording of "The Diary" on the air and then proceeded to make mincemeat out of me and the song.

"This record has no beginning and no end," Marty accused.

Kirshner, trying to smooth things over, said, "What about Bobby Darin? His 'Splish, Splash' is very similar." "I don't like Bobby Darin either," Marty said.

After continued exchanges, I walked off in tears, re-
fusing to do his TV show for which I was scheduled
that evening. When I got back to the hotel that night, I
turned the TV on, just to get Faye's reaction. He was
not finished with me yet. He related some of our conversation from that afternoon, played part of "The
Diary," and informed the audience I was too frightened
to come on. They roared with laughter. He then proceeded to knock me and my record to the ground.

Three days later, the local Chicago sales reports
came out from RCA Victor. "The Diary" had sold
40,000 copies since the Marty Faye show. He'd unwit-
tingly promoted the sale of the record, casting me as
underdog to a sympathetic Chicago audience.

Despite this impressive debut, "The Diary" leveled
off at number 22 in *Cash Box* and number 14 in *Billboard*. The song was good but had a limited appeal.
What it did, however, was establish me as a recording
star. In the 1950s a number 22 position meant over
500,000 copies sold. I was still giving all my royalties
directly to Mother.

PART II

THE RISE TO THE TOP
1957-1963

CHAPTER 9
OH, CAROL

Mom was having an affair and not bothering to lie to my father. At first Ronnie and I were shocked and expected an imminent breakup of the marriage. The amazing thing was that Mac Sedaka didn't seem to mind.

"Skinny," Dad said to Mom, "as long as you're being taken to nice restaurants and it's not costing me anything, I don't mind."

"I wasn't going to let you children know until you were completely grown," Mom said to me and Ronnie.

"Oh, that's okay, Mom," I said. "I always knew you were a woman ahead of your time. There is something I need to tell *you* about, though. I'm going steady with Leba Strassberg. She lives in Monticello, a few miles from her mother's hotel, the Esther Manor."

"Couldn't you find a nice Brooklyn girl?"

"Mom, I'm in love with Leba. But she's two-and-a-half hours away. Don't you think it's time I bought my first car?"

"So, buy it."

"On an allowance of $50 a week?"

"I'll issue a special check from the fund," Eleanor said.

My first car was a white 1959 Chevy Impala, a souped-up convertible with every extra you can imagine. I decided to show it off by driving Leba to her high school prom. On prom night Leba and I were having a great time until I sensed resentment from the Monticello High School prom crowd. It started with snide comments about the "rock 'n' roll star" going out with Leba and continued into the night. A couple of wise guys even threw coins at my feet, sarcastically paying "tribute."

I guess they were jealous of my newly gained name in music circles—and envious of the money they thought I made. After the prom was over, Leba and I headed for the car. When we got there I discovered the hubcaps had been stolen. I was terrified. Never having owned a car before, I had no mechanical ability whatsoever, and had no idea how a car worked. I thought the car wouldn't run without the hubcaps. I ran back to the kids I thought had taken them, and demanded my hubcaps back, but they all played dumb. In desperation I tried to start the car without the hubcaps. I gave the biggest sigh of relief in my life when I realized as I drove home that the wheels weren't going to fall off.

* * *

The biggest nightmare of every record star is to be a one-shot artist, to have only one hit record. With much trepidation Howie and I sat down to write a follow-up to "The Diary" called "Crying My Heart Out for You." It was written in the same style as "The Diary." When "Crying" was released, it only climbed to number 89 and I thought, oh my God, am I that one-shot artist? When Howie and I planned our next song we decided that I needed a drastic departure from the rock 'n' roll ballad and proceeded to write ourselves a key-pounding, exciting Chuck Berry-type song called "I Go Ape." It even had Jerry Lee Lewis piano fills. Howie's lyrics were very clever, including jokes about monkeys and chimpanzees and the monkey business my honey brought out in me. RCA Victor made no comment but agreed to release it.

On a TV show called "Peter Potter's Rate the Record," a panel of judges reviewed new records. By chance I happened to turn it on the night "I Go Ape" was about to be reviewed. If the judge liked the song he would ring a bell, and if he hated it he would push a button that made an obnoxious buzzer noise. The four judges were unanimous—the buzzer sounded four times. "I Go Ape" was just not typical Neil Sedaka. It seemed that after only two records audiences were trying to put me in a box and categorize me. RCA's promotion department released the record to the disc jockeys. They were underwhelmed. Apparently there had been an expression during World War II, "I go ape-shit," which the DJs disapprovingly thought the title was a play on.

I went to L.A. for a last attempt to promote "I Go Ape." Helen Weigand, the RCA local representative and a delightful lady, met me at the airport. She had arranged an audition for me with the Dinah Shore TV program. After singing "I Go Ape" at the audition, I explained to the director what a great production number it could be, with monkeys hanging from trees, and Tarzan swinging on a rope. Such a salesman! The director said don't call us, we'll call you, and that was the end of that. "I Go Ape" climbed as high as number 42 on the charts, but once again it was a disappointing showing.

Paradoxically, the same year the song became a smash all over Europe, especially in England, making my name practically a household word there. This success was of little help to me in America, however. RCA Victor had lost money over my last two singles and they were ready to drop me. Al Nevins talked them into one more release.

I knew I had to have a hit. I would get no more chances. Some days later, sitting at my desk, I picked up the current issue of *Billboard* magazine and turned to the page headlined "Hits of the World." This was a compilation of the Top 10 records in every major country in the free world. The top three in each country were almost always the same. Suddenly an idea hit me. I ran out and bought each of the three records, listening to them over and over again, analyzing what they had in common. I discovered they had many similar elements: harmonic rhythm, placement of the chord changes, choice of harmonic progressions, similar instrumentation, vocal phrases, drum fills, content, even the timbre of the lead solo voice. I decided to write a song that incorporated all these elements in one record.

It took me two-and-a-half hours to write the rough draft of the melody. For the first time since "The Diary" I was fussy and self-critical and I reworked the song many times. Finished at last, I called Howie Greenfield, who lived across the hall, and played him the melody.

"I want this to be an ode to my old high school girl-friend, Carol Klein [King]," I said. "I like the title 'Carol.'"

Howie wrote the first draft of the lyrics in twenty minutes. I grabbed the pages out of his hand and said, "There'll be no rewriting this time." I liked it at once. Howie looked at me in amazement as I sang his rough lyrics, "Oh, Carol, I am but a fool. Darling I love you, tho' you treat me cruel."

"Neil," Howie said, "you've got to be kidding. Let me polish it."

"This is exactly what I want. This is exactly what the song needs. A song can be ruined by too much pol-ishing."

I got together with an orchestrator, Chuck Sagle, and we planned the record in detail. The recording session at RCA Victor went smoothly except for one prob-lem—the "readers" once again sang too prettily. Nevins stopped the session for a meeting.

"What are we to do?" I asked. Fortunately, Chuck Sagle had a number of friends visiting in the studio, among them three teenage girls, nonsingers. Nevins got them up to the microphone, and I taught them an easy part—a unison-line intro, a middle section, and a coda, all variations on the same musical phrase. Al switched on the recording machine and the girls began to sing. They sounded rough, but right for the part. I improvised a spontaneous recitation, which brought Howie running to the studio in outrage after the take was over.

"That's an embarrassing rendition," he said. "It emphasizes the rough state of my lyrics. I'm ashamed of it."

"How many Carols in America want to hear just this sentiment?" I asked. "I think quite a few."

I finished the session satisfied. A friend of Leba's in the studio ran to the phone to call her, and when Leba asked how "Oh, Carol" turned out, she reported what had happened and said, "Either you'll love it or you'll hate it."

The record was released in 1959. This time my mother joined me on the promotional tour. Donnie Kirshner, who had recently married, remained at home. We began in San Francisco, where there was *no* air play. We went on to Texas—still no air play despite my usual visits to radio stations, record hops and retail stores. Perhaps I had lost the DJs forever with "I Go Ape." Mom tried to persuade me to turn "Oh, Carol" over and promote the B side, "One Way Ticket to the Blues," but I was still convinced "Oh, Carol" could be a hit.

It only takes one DJ or program director to create a hit record, and with "Oh, Carol," that DJ was to be Howard Miller of Chicago. When Mom and I walked into his private office, Howard played "Oh, Carol" and said nothing. He put the record on again and picked up the needle in the middle of the song. "My God," he said, "this is a hit. I love it." That was the turning point for "Oh, Carol"—and for me, because after "Oh, Carol" something came into being known as the Sedaka sound.

Mom and I flew back home, and that week "Oh, Carol" began to hit the airwaves in New York City. To celebrate I bought a Thunderbird convertible and roared across Brooklyn, turning the radio up full blast everytime "Oh, Carol" came on. I confess it's a great feeling, hearing yourself on the radio with a smash record.

"Oh, Carol" hit the charts at number 92. Martin Bloch played *Billboard's* Top 40 every Saturday morning, and each week I tuned in, hearing "Oh, Carol" slowly rise to the top. My competition was the tremendous "Mack the Knife" by Bobby Darin. "Oh, Carol" finally topped off at number 3. Not number 1, but close enough.

Just for fun, I went back to Lincoln High to visit. Some friends of mine were in the high school "Sing," and I sat quietly in the back of the auditorium, trying not to be seen. Within a few minutes, word spread that I was in the audience and all hell broke loose. Years before, when I was in the Catskill Mountains, I had once lied to a group of kids, telling them I was Danny of Danny and The Juniors, a group that sang the hit song "At the Hop." I'd wanted to see how it felt to be famous. Now I knew—it was like living a dream.

When Al Nevins gave me the worldwide reports on "Oh, Carol," I was in the top three in almost every country in the world. My research had paid off. Sales were approaching three million copies all around the world, and RCA Victor was delighted.

When my first check arrived for "Oh, Carol," I was so excited that I misread the amount. I ran to Mom waving the check in the air, crowing about $6,900. Mom studied the check and informed me I had in fact made $69,482.50.

In 1959, a few years later, Carole King recorded an answer on Decca called "Oh, Neil." It got a limited amount of air play. However, it is a collector's item and you can still hear it on the radio every so often. The lyric goes:

Oh Neil, I've loved you for so long
I would never dream you'd put me in a song.
I'm Carol, and I live in Tennessee,
I never thought that you'd remember me.

CHAPTER 10
ADIOS VIRGINITY

When Howie and I sat down to begin the task of writing the follow-up to "Oh, Carol," panic and fear gripped me. I listened to every record that was released in the coming months, searching for direction. I had to use some of the elements of "Oh, Carol," certainly, but I wanted to change the tempo. I finally wrote a melody that incorporated a two-voice section, where I would sing two different lines. I could then record the two lines, one track at a time, and mix them. Like "Oh, Carol," the song had an intro, a melody, and a coda. In fact, from there on, all my songs had this format. I called them "sandwich songs": the melody was the meat and the intro and coda the bread. The new melody I had composed had a danceable tempo. I always considered this so important that I would get up and dance after the last take to make sure it was danceable. Howie married the lyrics to the song with ease. We called it "Stairway to Heaven."

Rather than just writing songs, I was now starting to write records. As I composed on the piano, my left hand represented the bass line, and my right hand contained the sweeteners—the string lines or other melodic instruments. My midrange piano playing gave me the basic rhythm section—guitar, drums and percussion. My voice was a separate instrument, carrying the melody. It was distinctive, emphasizing the Sedaka sound—cutting, high, articulate, and most important of all, unmistakable. Being a classically trained musician, I could write more complex harmonic chord changes than most songwriters, taking pains with my choice of chords, intent on making the music more substantial than the popular bubblegum tune of the time. I was aiming for a more sophisticated audience. With Roy Orbison, Buddy Holly and I, sex appeal was not the key. We sold records because our songs were musiçally solid and had more than four chords.

"Stairway to Heaven" was easy to record. The studios in those days had only three tracks. My voice and piano were almost always in the middle track. If I were to sing with myself on a multivoice, or voice-over, it had to be bounced onto another track, left or right. Little by little I incorporated voice-overs in my work, and, like Les Paul and Mary Ford before me, became a big exponent of the technique.

"Stairway to Heaven" reached the Top 10 in America and Europe in 1959. Nevins and Kirshner decided to book me for my first live performance. The place they picked for my debut was a tiny club in Haddonfield, New Jersey, called The Smart Spot. My entire family and many of my friends were in the audience. On my first night I was a wreck, and having my family there didn't help. Singing with a small back-up group, I did many of my own songs. I wasn't very good.

For one thing, my repertoire was limited. And never having taken singing lessons, I did not use my voice properly. I was always afraid it would crack—and it did, many times. I only lasted a few nights. Performing, I discovered, is a separate art form unto itself, and developing into a performer takes years of practice and work.

Nevins was not anxious to book me as a performer again. "Neil, I'm sorry—I'm just scared to death that your record sales will stop after people see you performing."

It would also jeopardize his position as music publisher. The publishing was much more lucrative to him and Kirshner than the management was. If Al Nevins had had his way, he'd have locked me in a room and had me just continue to write. But I knew the records wouldn't last forever without personal appearances.

"Al, I'm just a voice on a recording. The only way I can sustain myself is to be up onstage. I need the experience, the chance to perform in front of people."

At last we compromised—Al booked me in Brazil, figuring it wouldn't matter if I flopped that far away. The Brazilians offered $8,500 per week, thanks to the success of "Oh, Carol." Dad went to Sao Paolo with me—an eighteen-hour flight on a propeller plane that left me in bad physical shape. When we arrived I was scared to death since I'd never been out of the U.S. before, I didn't know if my voice would hold, and I was terrified of working with foreign musicians.

At the airport there were thousands of people, both on the tarmac and inside the terminal. My father and I wondered what celebrity they were after until we saw huge signs saying "SALIDAS SEDAKA"—Welcome Sedaka. Screaming mobs started singing "Oh, Carol" in Portuguese.

Representatives of the promoter and my record company tried to keep me from being trampled, whisking me into one car, while my father was shoved into a second. A stranger from the promoter's staff took off with my music in a third.

Suddenly I panicked. My music was precious—it contained the orchestration for all seven songs. Without it, I was lost—I couldn't go on. I arrived at the hotel half an hour later, but my father and music were nowhere in evidence. Turning on the television in frustration I saw an advertisement for my forthcoming theater engagement. Outside the window hundreds of fans were milling in the street, hoping for a glimpse of me. It seemed that the only previous American singers to appear in Brazil had been Sammy Davis, Jr. and Nat King Cole. Brazil had heard about rock 'n' roll and they were ready. My Latin looks—dark hair and complexion—won me brownie points in Brazil.

My father and my music, caught in a traffic jam, finally arrived a few hours later, to my immense relief, but by now I was beginning to lose my voice from anxiety, the long trip and lack of sleep. That night I tossed

and turned fitfully, constantly rearranging the order of
the seven songs that comprised my show.

I woke up the next morning without a voice. The
promoter took me to a drugstore, where they gave me
an injection of some kind. I walked out and fainted on
the street. The promoter, seeing his money fly out the
window, picked me up and carried me back to the
hotel. Luckily, I had a day to recuperate.

My performance in Brazil was being televised na-
tionally. A few minutes before I went on camera, I
asked my translator to give me a couple of expressions
in Portuguese, something colloquial that would establish a rapport with the Brazilian public. The translator
said, "Tudo azul"—Real hip, crazy man, AOK—and
"Muito obrigado"—Thank you very much, I'm happy
to be here. The audience roared when I mispronounced
both phrases, but they appreciated the gesture. The
show went over, and suddenly I was an overnight sensation, the new sex symbol of Brazil with women chas-
ing me everywhere.

Rock stars are supposed to be great lovers, and at last
I had a chance to prove myself. In Curitiba, the next
city on the tour, the hotel manager arranged a surprise
for me—a young girl.

As I entered my room I saw her lying naked on the
bed, waiting for me. Her breasts were small, but well-
shaped, with dark, pert nipples. She was young but had
a sexy body which immediately aroused me.

"Do you speak English?" I asked her. She nodded
her head yes.

Up to this time I had never had sexual intercourse. At
last I was about to lose my virginity. But I felt bothered

by the circumstances—losing my cherry to a strange hooker in Brazil. It felt so impersonal. I wanted to back out, but I didn't want to insult the hotel manager. I sat down on the bed next to her, feeling embarrassed. I wasn't sure how to take the first step.

"What's your name?" I asked.

She reached out a hand and rubbed my crotch. "Letitia," she said.

"How long have you been doing this?" I asked, stalling.

"All my life," she replied in broken English.

"Do you always enjoy it?" I asked.

"It depends on the man."

With that comment I suddenly lost my erection. She put my hand on her breast, but nothing seemed to work.

"Just give me a minute," I said, trying to collect myself. I fled to the bathroom to take off my clothes.

Once in the bathroom I locked the door and tried to talk myself into it. At last I took off my clothes. Hurrying back to the bedroom, I quickly got under the sheets with her.

"I wanted to make fork with you since I first hear your voice on the radio," she said.

I grabbed awkwardly for her, hoping she would show me what to do. The room was fully lit—it was the middle of the afternoon. I felt no tenderness, no emotion. It was very cut and dried. After some clumsy foreplay I managed to get an erection again and started to rub myself against the hairs between her legs. I tried entering her several times without success and then I was in—and then it was all over, in a total of two minutes. I went back to the bathroom feeling empty and disheartened. My first sexual experience was a turkey.

The music side of the tour was more auspicious. Dances were held all over Brazil called *Bailes do Cupido*—Dances of Cupid—large record hops in honor of my "Estupido Cupido." My picture was on the cover of every major magazine in Brazil, and I had the number 1 and number 2 records in the country. When my father and I got to Rio, *Manchete* magazine ran a big story entitled "Sedaka Dethrones Elvis in Brazil." I finished my Brazilian tour with a TV special in Rio. The Brazilians had truly taken me to their hearts.

The next stop on the tour was Buenos Aires, Argentina. When our plane landed the local RCA representative there told me I had the country's top three songs: "Oh, Carol," "Stupid Cupid," and "Stairway to Heaven." I played the big football stadium before an audience of 86,000 people, an Argentinian record. I was finding my way as a performer at last.

Mac, my father, was putting my success to work for him. Dad was always a letter writer and enjoyed corresponding with my fans all over the world—so effectively that several young women showed up on our Brooklyn doorstep, suitcase in hand. In the beginning of my courtship with Leba, Mac had even decided to write her and sign my name.

CHAPTER 11
THE HIT FACTORY

As a teenage tunesmith I traveled into Manhattan's Tin Pan Alley every day on the old BMT subway line. I got on at Brighton Beach, the first station on the line, and got off at Fifty-ninth Street, about a forty-minute ride.

The original Brill Building, home of American popular music, was 1619 Broadway. Eventually that whole radius of blocks became known as Tin Pan Alley or the Brill Building area. Howie Greenfield and I wrote at 1650 Broadway, and it was there that most of the pop songs were written in the fifties and sixties.

At Aldon Music we wrote every day for at least five hours. Each team had its own cubicle containing a piano. Howie Greenfield and I, having scored the biggest hits, were given the luxury of a room with a window. Down the hall we could hear Carole King and

Eleanor and Mac with Ronnie and me
growing up in Brooklyn

My Lincoln High School
yearbook picture

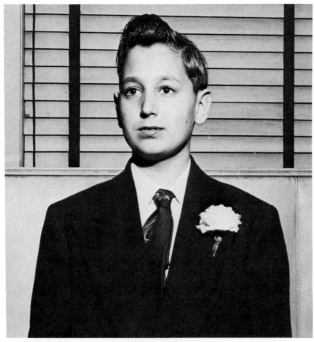

My Bar Mitzvah

With childhood friend and neighbor Carole Gold

With high school sweetheart Carol Klein (who later became Carole King), holding the songsheets for our hit records "Oh Carol" and "Oh Neil"

After reaching No. 1 in
Hit Parader and *Billboard*
with "Oh Carol" and
"Breaking Up Is
Hard to Do"

My first car, a white Chevy Impala. Ronnie's on the right

With my father Mac Sedaka in Texas
(Ethel Bennett)

In Buenos Aires during my first tour to South America

With Leba on our wedding day, September 11, 1962

Dara and Marc growing up in Brooklyn
(photo taken by their Daddy)

With Leba and Carol Bayer (yet to be Sager) and friend

With my longtime lyricist Howard Greenfield
entertaining at a party. Dionne Warwick, Leslie Uggams
and Allan Carr in the background
(Peter C. Borsari)

With lyricist Phil Cody

With Leba and close friends Maurice Gibb of The Bee Gees
and his wife Yvonne
(© 1982 by Bob Sherman/Camera 5)

The Sedaka family sailing home from London on the *Q.E.2*

Gerry Goffin putting together songs like "Locomotion," and brand new sounds were also emanating from the cubicles of Barry Mann, Cynthia Weill, Jack Keller, Hank Hunter, Paul Simon and Helen Miller. We soon became known as The Hit Factory. We had the hottest writers in the business under one roof, with dozens of hits on the charts.

At the end of the day we'd congregate at Hanson's, a coffee shop on the corner of Fifty-second Street and Seventh Avenue. We used to stop in and talk shop over a cup of coffee. Bobby Darin was a regular and a good friend. After hitting it big with "Splish Splash" he arrived at Hanson's one day with Harriet Wasser, his secretary and biggest fan. I was at Hanson's chatting with Tony Orlando, Don Kirshner, Howie, Carole and Gerry and Steve Brant, the teenage columnist.

When the others cleared out Bobby came over to our table to tell us about a new record he was cutting, "Dream Lover." I got so excited that he invited me to come to the recording studio with him the next day. "Great, I'll take the train in and meet you at the studio."

Bobby said, "Neil, there's something I don't understand. Here you are, a member of the songwriting royalty of your time, and you're still riding the subway. Hit records throw off a lot of money."

"Yes, but my mother handles all that. I don't see any of the money. She pays for the bills and then I'm given $50 a week for spending money."

Bobby remained silent, intent on stirring his coffee.

The next day I joined Bobby Darin and his musicians as they worked on "Dream Lover." After one

passage on the piano, I said, kidding, "Save this section
for me."

Bobby took me literally. "Why don't you play piano
for 'Dream Lover,' Neil? That sounded great."

"Sure," I said. "And why don't you put the guitar
licks up an octave?"

Bobby tried it that way and beamed a big smile at
me.

I ended up playing on "Dream Lover" and on the B
side did a solo piano section on a song called "Bull
Moose," which was about a piano player.

After Howie and I wrote each day, we then played
our songs for each other in Don Kirshner's big executive office. We lived and breathed music. We slaved
over our songs; it was not like the movies, with ideas
flashing in the middle of the night. Some days the creative juices really flowed, but other days were a struggle,
with nothing to show for hours of labor. It was a challenge for Howie and me to see how good we could be.
We kept trying to improve, to progress, creating new
phrases, interrhymes, extended bars, unusual chord
changes, beautiful melodic lines, hooks and catchy
lines.

In the beginning we were actually writing a song a
day. I usually came up with a melody first, or a good
portion of one, sitting at the piano, and singing out
tunes by trial and error. I continued to study the current hits, keeping in touch with what the public wanted
to hear. I especially loved to compose with a particular
singer's style in mind, such as Fats Domino, Chuck
Berry, the Everly Brothers and the New York doo-wop
groups like The Channels and The Nutmegs. I usually

went to Howie with at least two or three melodies so he could choose his favorites. Then he began fitting words to the music. Many times Howie wanted to alter a section of the melody. Other times I came up with lyrics. We knew quickly if a piece was good enough to devote time to and finish. More than one attempt wound up in the wastepaper basket.

Sometimes we fought bitterly and egos got in the way. But we always forgot and forgave when the song was finished. Success brought more confidence and, in turn, better songs.

CHAPTER 12
CALENDAR GIRL

Carole King married Gerry Goffin and went to work on her classic "Will You Still Love Me Tomorrow" for The Shirelles. She came into the studio every day with her newborn baby strapped to her back to conduct the session. I was in Don Kirshner's office the day Carole came in to hear the finished version.

"Carole, this is a masterpiece," I said. Everyone else agreed. The song went on to become one of the great pop standards.

Having a hit on both sides of a record is a special thrill for a songwriter. Here's how it happened for Howie and me. Al Nevins decided the A side of our new record would be "You Mean Everything to Me" with a cute little country-and-western piece, "Run,

Samson, Run," on the B side. I was planning to sing "Everything" on the Dick Clark show when, ten minutes before air time, Don Kirshner came running up to me. "Nashville and Memphis have been playing the B side, 'Run, Samson, Run.' They love it."

"I'll do both songs on the show," I told him, and I found myself with a two-sided hit, both appearing on the charts simultaneously. "Everything" reached number 19 and "Samson" went to number 28. Kirshner told me the only previous artists with two-sided hits were Elvis, Connie Francis, Rick Nelson and Brenda Lee. I was in very good company, but a bit disappointed. The record sales were split, and instead of having one Top 10 song, I had two Top 30s. Half the country was playing one side, and half the other.

Our next song, "Calendar Girl," was a rousing blockbuster from its conception. Howie's lyrics were unique—it took the listener through each month of the year. He got the title from an old movie listing in *TV Guide*. When I played it on the piano, I knew we were home free. It was an obvious hit. All I had to do was to capture the magic in the recording. Unfortunately, this was easier said than done. It was a tough song to record, balancing the rocking drumbeat section with the lyrical chorus lines. We did twenty-six takes over a three-hour period. The mixing was frustrating. But at last, "Calendar Girl" took shape. It was released in 1961 and became an instant smash, reaching number 4 on the charts.

It was the heyday of rock 'n' roll and Alan Freed's "Brooklyn Paramount Show" was a sensation. I was to

be one of three headliners, along with my old friend
Brenda Lee and Bobby Rydell. Bobby Vinton was the
band leader. There was one other act on the show, a
fantastic guitar player by the name of Bo Diddley. His
music was so hypnotic that audiences wouldn't let him
off the stage and automatically booed the next act. Mr.
Pleshette, the theater manager (and Suzanne Pleshette's father), said to me at rehearsal, "I want you to
follow Bo Diddley." I couldn't believe my misfortune.
I told Leba, who came to the rehearsal, "I hope Bo
Diddley has an accident." A half hour before the first
performance, they announced, "Bo Diddley has broken
his leg and will be unable to perform." For a moment I
thought I had a pipeline to heaven.

But even Bo Diddley's accident wasn't enough to
save me. The Brooklyn Paramount attracted a real
leather crowd, and before long lit cigarettes and beer
cans were being thrown at me. The crowd came to hear
the doo-wop groups, not Neil Sedaka.

Nevins and Kirshner once again sent me out of the
country, this time for a tour of the Far East—Japan and
the Philippines. The big hit in Japan in 1959 was "One
Way Ticket to the Blues," the B side of "Oh, Carol."
"Ticket" was written by Jack Keller and Hank Hunter.
I usually didn't do other people's material, but I fell in
love with the song at Aldon. They had promised it to
Frankie Avalon, but I coaxed them into letting me
record it. It was such a crowd-pleaser in Japan that I
had to open and close my concerts with "Ticket." They
called it "The Choo-Choo Train Song."

The Japanese people were convinced that Sedaka
was a Japanese name, and before my arrival they

slanted my eyes on all the posters and advance publicity. What a sight—a Sephardic Jew on a billboard in
the middle of the Ginza with slanted eyes. Before long
the daily papers carried Japanese caricatures of me.

The tour was moderately successful, thanks to my
friend and promoter, Tats Nagashima, but record sales
were far more successful than the concerts. "One Way
Ticket" held at the number 1 position in Japan for several months.

I had better luck as a performer in Manila, the next
stop on the tour, packing in 30,000 people each night.
Back in New York, Al Nevins said the time was right
for me to put together a formal cabaret act and go for
major exposure. A special writing team composed and
choreographed the material I would use, and an orchestrator made up the charts. Except for a small medley of
my own songs, the repertoire consisted of standard arrangements of such songs as "Summertime," "Comes
Love," "The Twelfth of Never," and an elaborate piece
called "I Can't Say No to a Piano," incorporating a toy
piano. We rehearsed in a studio for weeks. I was taught
how to work a microphone, how to move and conduct
myself onstage. For the last two rehearsals we brought
in the full orchestra—fourteen members, including my
own drummer who traveled with me.

We decided to break in the act at Three Rivers Inn at
Syracuse, New York. There would be no press, just a
glorified dress rehearsal in front of a small audience.
The gig cost a fortune in those days—over $20,000 be-
tween the musical scores and the fees and hotel rooms.
I hoped it was worth it.

The opening night the audience numbered about

twenty people, mostly friends and family. As I feared, the act was a disaster. The pacing was bad. There were no peaks in the performance, no dynamics. Everything sounded the same—boring. I forgot lines and began to sweat. My voice did not hold up well. Eddy, the drummer, panicked and started to rush the tempos, and the band drowned me out. The audience applauded politely, but I have never felt so embarrassed in my life and I couldn't wait to get offstage. The act was just not me.

Although I was making $5,000 a week as a performer, it seemed to me I needed new management. Aldon was taking twenty-five percent of my fees as my manager but this was a drop in the bucket compared to the publishing business. When I asked for a release from my management contract, Al Nevins and Kirshner agreed to call it quits. It cost me $25,000 to buy my way out. The word got out and calls started coming in from the top personal managers in the business.

My Mom kept telling me to hold off.

The next time I saw Bobby Darin, he said, "You're making a big mistake."

"Whatever happens, I can't hurt Mom."

Being a loyal son, I continued to ignore calls from the top managers. As a result my life changed drastically. I wasted my time playing dives in Brooklyn. I should have realized that I had made a grave mistake by not meeting with professional managers. I played small-time, tiny clubs where I received no New York coverage in the papers.

My songwriting, though, continued to prosper. I had

two more Top 10 records with "Little Devil" and "Happy Birthday Sweet Sixteen."

One day I was in Hanson's when it was jammed with the big songwriters of the late fifties and early sixties—Helen Miller, Barry Mann, Cynthia Weill, Hank Medress, Jack Keller and Hank Hunter—and we were all jabbering joyously to Bobby Darin about the musical coup he'd just scored. He had started by writing great rock 'n' roll songs like "Splish Splash" and "Dream Lover" and now had made an incredible transition with "Mack the Knife."

Bobby smiled at me and said, "Remember 'Dream Lover,' Neil? When you played the piano, you gave the record a shot."

CHAPTER 13

BREAKING UP IS HARD TO DO

During one of my Los Angeles promotional tours, I happened to hear a local hit on the radio called "It Will Stand" by The Showmen. It fascinated me. There was something about the sound of the lead singer's voice that haunted me. As I traveled from city to city, the record sounded different in each place, almost as if the change of scenery altered the mood. "It Will Stand" seemed like a prophecy. I went back to New York and tried to capture the same kind of enthusiasm and mood in a song of my own. The melody came to me in a flash, and the title seemed an inspiration—"Breaking Up Is Hard to Do." It was unusual for me to write lyrics or titles, but somehow the entire composition of the song seemed predestined.

Then I hit my first stumbling block. When I took the song and title into Howie, he was not enthusiastic.

"We're in the middle of a song already," he reminded me. "Listen, put this new inspiration of yours aside. I'm sure it will keep."

The following week I tried Howie again, and this time he was more receptive. The lyrics began to unfold:

> Don't take your love away from me.
> Don't you leave my heart in misery,
> If you go, then I'll be blue.
> Breaking up is hard to do.

As it took form, every step felt so right, as if somehow it had happened before. So was the case with the bridge and the middle section. Automatically, and spontaneously, I sang out the bridge:

> They say that breaking up is hard to do.
> Now I know, I know that it's true.
> Don't say that this is the end.
> Instead of breaking up
> I wish that we were making up again.

It had a wonderful chord change that seemed to flow. It was simple, yet original. It was the first time in rock 'n' roll that a minor seventh chord was used.

That week Howie and I finished three songs. As usual, at the end of the week I sang my new songs for the various writers in the office. The others were particularly interested in the direction my writing was taking as I was the most successful songwriter at Aldon. Strangely, of the three songs I played for Barry Mann and Cynthia Weill that week, "Breaking Up" was their least favorite. But there was something about it that intrigued *me*, even from its infancy.

A recording session was set up for "Breaking Up Is Hard to Do." The night before the session I couldn't fall asleep. A piece of the puzzle was still missing. The song was not quite right. As I lay awake that night, I realized "Breaking Up" needed an obbligato line running through the song. Up until that point, my past songs had had only touches of obbligato lines. They took the form of doo-be-doos and tra-la-las. This had become my trademark. Suddenly out of the blue, a line came to me. I immediately called Allan Lorber, the arranger, and woke him up. "Neil, it's 12:30, what do you want? We have a recording session tomorrow."

"I'm sorry Al. But I just had a great idea for 'Breaking Up Is Hard to Do'—an obbligato line. Listen—" and I sang it to him. "Could you write up a guitar part throughout the song for tomorrow?"

"Neil, you've got to be kidding."

"Please, Al—it's important."

Al, pro that he was, agreed.

The next morning I picked up the background singers, a group called The Cookies, in Coney Island. I had been using them on several singles records. They were the group that recorded my very first record on Atlantic, "Passing Time." As we drove to the studio, I taught them the obbligato line that had come to me in the middle of the night and was destined to become one of the most famous of all time: *Down-Doo-Be-Doo-Down-Down, Comma, Comma.*

When we got to the studio, I compulsively took over the session, leaving Al Nevins in disbelief at the console. We still had only a three-track recording machine. I began recording the obbligato line on the first track. The band looked at me as if I was half crazy as I sang, for two and a half minutes, "Down-doo-be-doo-down-down, comma comma . . ." With each take, the volume of the previous track was made progressively weaker. I purposely saved the lead for last, so it would be the most audible. But Nevins and the band didn't know that. They had no idea what I was doing. I looked up at Al Nevins and said, "Trust me."

Al had not heard the obbligato line before the session, of course. He was delighted. "It has a Latin flavor to it," he commented.

After completing the recording of the obbligato line, I listened to the first playback in ecstasy. It sounded like the first part of an ingenious puzzle. When I recorded the last voice, the lead voice, the musicians started to tap their toes. "Breaking Up" was magic from beginning to end. The record session was over.

Even before the test pressing arrived at the office, Nevins kept telling me, "You've got something here, Neil." A few days before I left for a scheduled tour of England, "Breaking Up Is Hard to Do" came on over the car radio, and I knew then it was going to be solid gold.

My first concert in England was at the London Palladium, the most prestigious concert hall in England.

The day of the show I had butterflies and diarrhea and told my mother, who had accompanied me, "I'm not going on."

"Yes you are," she said. Opening night she stood with me in the wings and literally pushed me out on the stage, saying, "This is what you chose, Neil, and you'll do it. I told you to get a music Ph.D. and be a teacher. But you wanted to be a singer. So sing."

The English public was warmly receptive and the Palladium concerts were a turning point for me. For the first time in my career I was able to relax onstage.

Leba cabled me the astronomical sales figures of "Breaking Up" while I was in England. In one week, the record sold 64,000 copies on Monday, and 72,000 copies on Wednesday, equalling the sales figures of Elvis Presley. "Breaking Up" came on the American Top 100 at number 62, then moved to number 26, number 10, number 5, and then to number 3. I was still in England when I got the telegram telling me "Breaking Up" had reached number 1.

My first Number 1 record. I felt like jumping up and down and screaming in the hotel lobby. Ninety-nine other songs beneath it. I was at the top of the heap.

Unfortunately, as I was to discover, the thrill of success lasts just a few months. Then comes the terror of trying to follow it up. Success is tremendous, but it carries with it a curse—you've got to keep topping yourself.

I was still riding high when I returned to New York. Parties, fancy restaurants, the works. Nevertheless, I was reminded that hit records don't last forever. Watching other stars and their record careers, I realized that the normal period of top stardom lasted between four and five years. This was true with Brenda Lee, The Everly Brothers, Fats Domino, Gene Pitney, Roy Orbison, Rick Nelson and many others. But I was determined to stay at the top as long as I could.

CHAPTER 14
LEBA

Though Leba and I had been going together for four years, I was still dating other women as well. I thought I was too young, too awed by success to get married. Leba wanted marriage very much. As she had always been self-conscious about her nose—it had a bump on it, not unlike Barbra Streisand's—she was convinced that it was this that kept me from dating her exclusively. She wanted to have it fixed.

During a date at the Concord Hotel in the Catskills, we finally had a blow-up over our relationship.

"Fine," she yelled at me. "Don't marry me. But some day I'll walk in here with my husband—a famous doctor or lawyer—with my perfect nose, wearing my Christian Dior dress, and I'll sit in the audience applauding ever so politely while you're sweating it out up on that stage."

I didn't know what to say. Her family had never been thrilled with our romance, except for Leba's father Irving, who had decided I was a genius. Her mother Esther had offered Leba a trip to Europe to forget me. Leba's uncle, Carl Goldstein, was of the same mind. "What do you want with a musician?" he said to her. "How can you compare a doctor or a lawyer with a songwriter? You'll never be happy with him." But Leba loved me. She had even attended Community College in Brooklyn so that we could be near each other.

During one period when I hadn't seen Leba for several weeks because of performances and songwriting sessions, she came over unannounced. I found myself in for an incredible surprise. She had had her nose done. I almost didn't recognize her. She looked absolutely gorgeous. The change was more than just physical, though. Leba seemed different, more confident about herself and her life. She had always been beautiful, but I don't think she was aware of it.

I guess I must have been swayed by the nose job, because soon afterwards I made a very important decision. My other dates had meant nothing to me.

Calling her from a gig in Pittsburgh, I said, "I think we should get married."

"I think the phone's broken," she said.

I had to put Howie on the line to convince her I was serious.

The wedding took place at Esther Manor Hotel in

Monticello, New York, on September 11, 1962. Leba looked ravishing.

The reception was held at the Concord Hotel in the Catskills because we wanted Esther to be able to relax as a guest. Leba looked shocked rather than pleased when Mom approached us on the lawn, where we were sipping champagne, and we were informed that our "allowance" was being increased to $225 a week.

Mother said, "Of course, the whole honeymoon is paid for in advance and separate from the allowance. Here's your itinerary for a four-week European tour and these are your tickets for a transatlantic crossing on the Queen Elizabeth I."

That night, honeymoon shyness enveloped us. It was freezing outside, and there was no heat in our room. But we were too scared to complain. We huddled together for warmth.

The next morning we drove to Manhattan and boarded the Queen Elizabeth I for our four-week honeymoon in Europe. Friends and family greeted us with Earl Wilson's morning column—NEIL SEDAKA MARRIES CATSKILL MOUNTAIN HEIRESS.

On the voyage across the Atlantic I was able to forget music and work for once in my life and relax and enjoy dancing, swimming, movies, broth on the promenade deck, skeet shooting, gambling, fabulous food and, most of all, the love of my bride Leba. We swept through England, France, Spain and Switzerland in four weeks.

Now that my life contained the perfect love partner it seemed complete. Professionally I had been happy since I'd discovered the power of music. I tried to explain it to Leba as we sat having drinks at Le Flor, the sidewalk cafe on the Left Bank in Paris.

"When you're a songwriter, each day is a fascinating journey into the unknown world of creativity. Howie and I never know what will come out, if anything at all."

Leba smiled. "Songwriters are a special breed. It's something that sets you apart. You can create something out of thin air, something that can entertain friends, be recorded, make money and last forever."

"I like the feeling of power it gives me when I sing one of my songs and can tell from people's faces that I am putting them exactly where I want them to be emotionally."

"Or even making them jump up and dance. What can be better than making people happy, even if it's only for a moment."

"Or consoling them that life is about love and loss and sadness too."

We returned to the States and settled in a small apartment at 370 Ocean Parkway, a temporary residence. During the previous summer Mom and I had surprised Leba by taking a spacious two-bedroom apartment in a building, Seacoast Towers, under construction in Brighton Beach. Seacoast Towers, which was supposed to be finished in October, was not ready for occupancy, so our friends Bruce and Susan Morrow (he was the famous DJ Cousin Brucie) found us the temporary place which we were able to rent on a month-to-month basis.

When Mom and I drove up to Monticello with the news, I said, "Leba, I have a wonderful surprise for you. Mom and I just rented a beautiful apartment in Brighton overlooking the water. It's only a block away from Mom's house."

Leba looked less than pleased.

After a moment she said, "Brighton Beach? I was hoping we might look together for a small apartment in Manhattan."

At which point Mom looked unhappy at the prospect of us moving out of Brooklyn.

CHAPTER 15
LOVE AND MONEY

I was to play the Copacabana, one of the hottest night spots in New York—but not as a headliner, as an opening act. At Hanson's Coffee Shop Bobby Darin shook his head and said, "Neil you've got the number 1 record all over the world, and here you are, second banana to Jan Murray."

I was miserable. But fate stepped in—Jan Murray canceled, and I became the headliner. It ended up being a successful engagement.

I was still playing the Catskills, however, and I knew that I should be doing the big TV shows.

Eventually Ed Sullivan came through, and the week before I was to be on I was asked to attend the broadcast and sit in the audience. Ed Sullivan was going to introduce me and have me take a bow.

A newcomer named Barbra Streisand made her television debut that night. I had done a benefit with her some time before, at which Sophie Tucker was the mistress of ceremonies. Hearing Barbra sing "Cry Me a River," I knew she was going to be a superstar.

Towards the end of *The Ed Sullivan Show*, Ed announced, "Ladies and gentlemen, sitting in our audience tonight is the very popular teenage favorite from right here in Brooklyn, New York, a Juilliard graduate, singer Neil Sedaka. Let's hear it for Neil!" The audience broke into applause, and I took my bow. I guess the whole thing was a way of gearing the audience up for my appearance the next week.

I could not have been more apprehensive. Ed Sullivan had the biggest audience in TV, and the show was broadcast live. My performance would have to be perfect.

The night before I went on the Sullivan show Leba made a special dinner of fried chicken, one of my favorites. Biting into a drumstick I lost the cap on my front tooth.

"Oh my God," I moaned, "the Sullivan show is tomorrow. Is this some kind of omen?" We called our dentist in Brighton only to find out he had gone skiing for the weekend. Then we called our friend Bruce Morrow, who lived in the same building.

"I have a hysterical, toothless singer here," Leba told him. "He's got to be at the Sullivan show tomorrow morning for rehearsals. Would you know a dentist nearby?"

Bruce said, "I have a dentist on Ocean Parkway. Stay cool. I'll see if I can get him to come into his office."

Half an hour later, Bruce called. "He's on his way in. Have Neil meet him at his office."

Leba and I scurried downstairs to look for a cab. It was the middle of a winter snowstorm in New York, and Leba was afraid I would catch a cold in the snow and lose my voice. Dear Leba was seven months pregnant at the time, yet she told me, "You stand in the lobby, Neil. I'll go and find a cab."

Eventually we made it to the dentist and the tooth was replaced. I arrived at the Sullivan show early the next morning with an entire day of blocking, rehearsals and two performances ahead of me. The dress rehearsal was staged in front of an audience right before showtime that evening. Kaye Ballard and Nanette Fabray were the other guests, along with an assortment of monkeys, elephants and lions. I was to begin with a piece by Chopin on the piano, followed by "Calendar Girl" and closing with "Yiddisha Momma." I overheard Ed Sullivan tell an assistant, "I don't want that rock 'n' roll kid singing 'Yiddisha Momma.' It just doesn't fit." I was very disappointed—that was my show stopper. After much haggling, I was able to convince Bob Precht, the producer and Ed's son-in-law, to put it back in.

As the show started I noticed that whenever Ed Sullivan was on camera, a man followed him on the floor with a handheld spotlight, shining it up at his face. Supposedly he was attempting to make Ed more photogenic, but this tactic only encouraged more jokes from comedians about Ed Sullivan's great stone face.

It seemed like an eternity until Ed announced me. I stood backstage and emptied an entire soup machine, thinking, for some reason, that hot soup would calm me down.

The show went well. Leba—due to her pregnancy—and my sister Ronnie watched from home. They assured me that my nervousness didn't show, though I wasn't sure I believed them. Ed liked me enough to invite me back.

I was tinkering with the last bars of a new song I had been writing when my old friend Freddie Gershon came into the office. Freddie was now a successful show business lawyer—quite a change since our days in Brooklyn and at Juilliard. He was very well known for his creative ideas. Without so much as a "Hi, how've you been, Neil?," he demanded: "Play me the follow-up to 'Breaking Up Is Hard to Do' "—already assuming I had written it. Fortunately I had. I immediately launched into my new song, "Next Door to an Angel." Freddie went wild, clapping and shouting, "You've got another Top-10 hit on your hands."

A few weeks later I played the finished record of "Next Door to an Angel" for him and, although Freddie was a little disappointed with the production, his prediction had been right on target. In fact in the four years from 1959 to 1962, I was to have ten Top-10 records in a row, with sales totalling over 25 million copies.

How odd, then, that I never saw much in the way of money. Although I was happy with a new car now and then, Leba was not. My accountant for several years, Alan Klein, who later was to manage The Beatles at the time of their breakup, wanted me to invest in a building

in Birmingham, Alabama. My mother took a look at the
building and recommended the deal, so I bought it. I
never did see the building, but I wound up losing hundreds of thousands of dollars in the deal—the single
worst business investment of my life. I also noticed
some expensive jewelry my mother began wearing. I
assumed I was paying for it, but I didn't dare question it.

For some time Leba's cousin, Roberta, had been dating Al Nevins. She was seventeen and Al was fifty-
two. Roberta was the complete opposite of Leba. She
had the figure of a beautiful high-fashion model, but an
unpredictable personality. I had often been invited up
to Al's apartment on the East Side for parties, but now
we seemed to be frequenting there more than ever. Al,
the suave and sophisticated man of the world, gave fabulous parties, and many of the writers and performers
under contract to Aldon Music, such as Carole King,
Barry Mann, Tony Orlando and Tony Wine would,
during the course of a dinner party, play their newest
creations on Al's red-lacquered piano. Roberta also introduced me to such people as Lionel Bart, Joey Dee,
the new singing sensation, and Bob Crewe, the talented
producer-writer who produced Frankie Valli and The
Four Seasons. Leba and I often found ourselves guests
at some of the wildest parties in New York at Bob
Crewe's opulent triplex on Fifth Avenue, complete
with trees, a waterfall, mirrored ceilings, and an outdoor terrace that overlooked Central Park. I wasn't
used to such splendor and magnificence. The New
York party scene was heady wine.
  Al Nevins, however, was soon to give up the scene.

In 1963, he and Don Kirshner sold Aldon Music to
Screen Gems-Columbia for over $2 million. While Don
accepted an executive position with the company, Al
took his half of the money and left for Paris. I was sorry
to see him go. It had seemed only a short time before
that Howie and I had first walked into their offices and
found them still unpacking their boxes and setting up
shop.

In June of 1963 Leba presented me with something
to take my mind off Aldon Music. On the twenty-sixth,
she gave birth to our first child, a six-and-one-half-
pound girl, Dara Felice Sedaka. My sister Ronnie had
been warning Leba for the last several months that the
labor pains could be very rough.

"Leba, it's like a lion ripping out your insides," Ronnie said, thinking of her own difficult delivery.

Leba kept waiting for the lion but he never came.
When I finally suggested that we'd better go to the hospital, her labor pains were only a minute apart. At the
hospital she walked up to the admitting desk, completely erect, and filled out the paperwork. I was an absolute wreck. When she finished, she waved goodbye
and said, "See you soon."

An hour later Dr. Jack Golliger came downstairs,
saying, "Congratulations, Neil, it's a girl." Unable to
contain myself, a few minutes later I bolted up the
stairs, two steps at a time, and darted into the recovery
room. God knows how I even found it. I just wanted to
see Leba and sneak a glimpse of our child. But as I
opened the door, Dr. Golliger saw me and yelled, "Get
out of here with those dirty shoes."

"Yeah," Leba said from the bed, smiling. "Get out of here. This is my show. Today, I'm the star."

That morning I saw her in the nursery with all the other newborns, in their cribs behind a glass partition. She looked like a beautiful Korean doll.

We hired a nurse, Mrs. Easton, and a few days later Dara came home with us. Friends and family poured in to see our baby, including Susan and Bruce Morrow. Connie Francis sent a telegram: I AM SO HAPPY TO HEAR ABOUT THE ARRIVAL OF LEBA AND NEIL'S ALICE IN WONDERLAND. Connie was referring to my new single, "Alice in Wonderland," which had been released a few weeks before and had reached number 12.

A month after my daughter Dara's birth I set off for South America with my mother on tour. Leba was to be left behind with the baby. Although she felt that she could join me, it was considered bad for my teen-idol image for my wife to be along on these tours. This caused many tearful nights before I left.

Leba and I were now on a salary of $275 a week. The money was deposited each week by Mom in our checking account—$25 of which was put in our savings account. Leba and I had many discussions about this before I left. "It's as if we're children and she's paying our way. Frankly, I feel like we're playing house." We didn't even have our own credit cards.

The South American tour was a grind—night after night of concerts and cabaret. I also recorded two LPs in 1963 in Buenos Aires, a piano rendering of my compositions and a Spanish translation of my big hits for the Latin American market. After three weeks of constant work in Argentina, Chile and Peru, I flew directly to Rome for an extensive Italian tour.

The fact that I was tired and ill hit me with frightening force during the flight to Italy. I had to face the fact that I had overextended myself physically and might not be able to go on. I felt like I was getting bronchitis, and though I had learned to sing over a cold or sore throat, when it went into the bronchial tubes, I was always knocked completely out of commission. From the feeling in my lungs I could tell I was coming down with the worst. Out came the vaporizers, the Vicks, the salt water gargling and the hot tea and honey. This was before my drinking days—I was still only drinking Coca-Cola. Booze probably would have helped.

In this condition I arrived in Rome to be confronted immediately by a girl claiming she had love letters from me. She was seventeen and she was with her mother. The girl threw her arms around me and cried in Italian, "I love you, I love you." As I peeled her off me, she ecstatically pulled out a handful of love letters from her purse with my signatures on them. Inspecting one of the signatures, I realized what my father had been up to while handling my fan mail.

The girl and her mother followed me to my hotel as I tried to explain that I was not well. The girl was crying by now. "I own every Italian record you make," she wrote on a piece of paper for me, using an Italian-English dictionary. "I give everything in the world to be with you." At last I felt so sorry for her that I invited the girl and her mother up to my room for coffee. As gently as possible I explained that I had not written her the letters, that in fact I was a married man with a baby daughter. At last she understood, and left smiling happily after receiving autographed copies of some of my American records.

By this time I was ready to collapse, and I immediately went to bed to try to recover from the incredible fatigue and weakness that had overtaken me. The next day—the day of the concert—the promoter, Ricardo Cella, suggested I see a throat doctor. The doctor I went to, upon examining me, said it would be impossible for me to put on a performance. "It looks to me as if you might have typhoid," he said.

"Typhoid," my mother said, looking alarmed.

When I returned to the hotel we met Ricardo Cella to say there would be no concert in Rome. He was very upset. "You must have a doctor from the government to verify you are actually ill and not faking in order to get out of the concert." Altogether I was examined by three doctors. Each assured Ricardo that I was sick as hell.

I called Leba and broke the bad news.

"I think I have typhoid fever. I've had to cancel the concert in Rome."

Leba was so upset that she insisted on leaving Dara, who was a month old, in the hands of her mother, Esther, and flying to Rome at once. Leba never knew when I was slightly ill and exaggerating or when it was the real thing. Many times I didn't know, either. Often psychosomatic symptoms developed from nerves before a big concert. But this time I was really sick.

It wasn't typhoid after all but I did have a bad case of bronchitis.

"I'll take care of you," Leba crooned on joining me in Rome, and for the next several days she administered sympathy and chicken soup and copious doses of medicine.

I decided I was ready to continue with my next concert on the Italian Riviera. Mother remained in Rome, as she'd heard enough kvetching from me already. Leba and I and a road manager from Genoa boarded a train—Alitalia Airline was on strike—and then we continued by sports car on a seemingly never-ending winding road, whereupon Leba got sick.

Hours later we finally arrived in Riccione on the Italian Riviera. Although I felt much better, my voice was still not really ready for a performance. Nevertheless I decided to give the audience my best.

The venue was a large, outdoor night club. It was packed with Italian fans and members of the press. The night before the famous Italian singer Mina had sung, to thunderous applause. She was a tough act to follow.

The opening of the act went well—but within fifteen or twenty minutes my voice began to give out. I couldn't sing the high notes at all. I didn't know what to do. Embarrassed, without a word of explanation, I walked off the stage.

The audience thought it was a brief intermission. When the manager came running over to me, gesticulating wildly, I explained in broken Italian, with the help of my road manager, that I was ill and could not continue. His face turned ashen.

"Please," he begged. "Go out and play the piano for another hour. Anything. Mina sang for one and a half hours last night. If you don't do the same, there'll be a riot."

I knew that these people did not come to hear me play the piano. There would be a riot whether I played or not. Sadly, I had to refuse.

When the manager made the announcement, "Neil Sedaka is ill—I'm sorry to say that he cannot continue," the crowd filled the club with curses and catcalls. The three of us decided it would be a good time to leave . . . and fast. Running down a hill to get to our car, we saw members of the audience on the terrace of the club, cursing in Italian and screaming, "Get the *pomodori!*"

Pomodori, we immediately discovered, are tomatoes. Leba and I began to be pelted with them from above. In a few minutes we looked like we'd just been through a war.

The review the next day on the front page of the local paper read, "Could this be the same Neil Sedaka who sings so beautifully on records?" I had been billed as "The voice that makes you dream" because of my hit "I Must Be Dreaming." The review continued: "This is definitely not a voice that makes you dream. It is a voice that gives you nightmares."

Despite this indictment, I sold more than 3 million records in 1963 and 1964 in Italy, and I not only recorded songs in Italian while I was there, but also sang at the famed San Remo festival, where, in a reversal of situations, I was proclaimed a star.

PART III
THE CRASH TO THE BOTTOM
1964-1970

CHAPTER 16
DISASTER

By the end of 1963 pop music had changed drastically with the invasion of British rock 'n' roll—especially The Beatles. The music was completely different from mine. Beatlemania swept the world and fans couldn't buy enough records.

Over the next year my popularity diminished rapidly and groups like The Rolling Stones—antiestablishment, sexy, rebellious, crude—ascended to the top. They wore funky clothes, turned their backs on the audience, and drenched themselves in an aura of sex and drugs. It was exactly the opposite of what my music represented.

Slowly my record sales began to slip. "Let's Go Steady Again" only went as high as the 20s on the charts. "Bad Girl" never climbed higher than number

30, and "The Dreamer" was lucky to reach the 40s. "Sunny" made a brief appearance on the charts at 90.

And then nothing.

My records no longer made the charts at all. The air play stopped.

The big tours were over.

Although I thought I was prepared for such a situation, I found myself completely destroyed. People met me on the street, saying, "Didn't you used to be Neil Sedaka?" If they asked what I was doing, I told them I was in real estate. The balloon had burst, the dream was over.

Despite an attempt on my part to record the new style of rock, RCA would not promote it, and the public did not buy it. There was no fooling myself. I had had four years of spectacular success. Now I would have to be satisfied with writing music behind the scenes—or nothing at all.

Although I had made a great deal of money up to this time, I had saved very little, especially with the real estate fiasco. The old royalties continued to come in, but not anywhere near the amount I had made before. Leba was used to nice things, and I wanted desperately to give them to her. And I now had a family of three to support. When Don Kirshner and Screen Gems made me an offer as a staff writer, I accepted. They put me on salary—quite a difference from the money to be made from performing. Leba cashed in the bonds that were given to her as a child.

On the in-law front, Leba was getting more and more upset with the control Mom had over our finances, especially under our present circumstances. Leba brought up insurance policies, credit cards and unexplained gifts, at which point I lost my cool and said, "My mother would never cheat me. If you think so, you can get out."

At home I was in shock, paralyzed by the crisis which had the potential of wrecking my marriage. Howie and I continued to write together. We drove into New York five days a week, putting in five hours a day. At least the job was stable, and I was able to enjoy being a new father. Dara was delightful, and after all that traveling, it was blissful to be home with Leba. I was becoming resigned to my new life.

In the next several years Howie and I wrote a few successful songs. "Working on a Groovy Thing," written with Roger Atkins, was recorded by The Fifth Dimension. Both Tom Jones and The Fifth Dimension recorded our "Puppet Man." Tony Christie recorded "Amarillo" and the record sold over 2 million copies. "One Day of Your Life" was recorded by Andy Williams and "One More Ride of the Merry-Go-Round" by Peggy Lee.

One day Carol Bayer Sager walked up to me, flicking her beautiful eyelashes, and introduced herself.

"I write lyrics," she said. "Would you be interested in collaborating with me?"

I liked her spunk. We wrote together for quite a while, and although we had no great hits, the sessions with Carol Bayer Sager were inspiring. She seemed to get better with each song.

I was playing some real dives in Montreal, Quebec and Three Rivers. The pay was small. Some nights I remember playing to a handful of people—depressing, but I needed the money. Some nights I'd do three shows, having to shout over the noise of the drunks. I had a Canadian drummer named George Angers who was nice company, but for the most part the bands were lousy and the audiences were worse.

Leba and I still lived at Seacoast Terrace. During breaks in my writing, I often walked along the board-walk with friends and went to Nathan's in Coney Island and had clams on the half shell. We always passed the famous roller coaster—I still got a thrill watching those cars race up and down the tracks. I thought of the heights I'd reached so quickly in my career, and how I was now plummeting to the bottom. Maybe my fortunes would climb again.

My enthusiasm for life always kept me going, even in the darkest days. Leba looked at me and said, "The more excited you get over something, the more you seem to enjoy it. That childlike quality in you keeps you young." These were times when I desperately needed to hear that.

My sister Ronnie was equally supportive. She grabbed both my hands one night and talked at break-neck speed, without blinking her eyes once: "Happiness will be yours, Neil—contentment, peace of mind. Have patience. This plus more will come! That is what I wish for you—and as long as I am alive I will stand by you, through thick and thin—helping you in every way, with every nerve in my body—with my heart and soul. You can *always* turn to me—I will be there for you, no matter *what*."

I met Bobby Darin one day, and we got on the depressing subject of all the rock stars of the fifties and sixties who were dropping from the charts, as I was, like flies—gone were Bobby Rydell, Jimmy Clanton, Brian Highland, Frankie Avalon, Fabian, Lloyd Price, Fats Domino, The Everly Brothers, Tommy Roe, Tommy James, Tommy Sands, Bobby Vee, Brook Benton. Bobby Darin, however, had a big hit at the time—"If I Were a Carpenter." It was the last time I saw Bobby Darin alive. His young life and brilliant career were cut short by heart disease.

I hoped the other fallen rock stars had some of the consolations—some of the normal fulfillments of life—that were pulling me through the valley of despond. After a day at the office, I would come home to Leba, who had dinner ready. Later in the evening friends in the building would drop by, or we would entertain them at dinner parties.

I began to feel like a normal person again, doing things that everyone did, going to the movies with my wife and kids and playing paddle tennis in the Brighton Baths. This was the first time in our married life that I didn't have to pick myself up and travel to a gig.

One day at a dinner party with some friends I was passed a small hand-rolled cigarette. It was the newly popular drug, marijuana, and that night I smoked my first joint. Within a few minutes, I found I couldn't stop laughing. Everything was hilarious. And I noticed that when stoned, I lost many of my inhibitions. Upon experimenting a little, I discovered it was very effective in writing music. Although Leba didn't like it, I began to smoke every day, in the bathroom and on the terrace, before composing at the piano. More often than not, the

tunes were imaginative and fresh, so spontaneous the
songs came as a surprise to me, as if someone else's
music was coming out of me. It was a great creative
tool, although I almost never carried it over into my social life.

My sister Ronnie and her family—she now had two
sons, Barry and Gary—had just moved to a new neighborhood in Brooklyn, Mill Basin, when they came for a
big family get-together Leba and I were hosting at our
apartment in Seacoast Terrace. Mac said, "Sweetie, are
you making friends with your new neighbors?"

"You know me, Dad," Ronnie said. "I hate to go
around ringing doorbells to make friends, though I'd
love to. I just don't know how."

Mac looked at me with a wink and a smile and then
turned back to Ronnie and said, "Don't you worry
about a thing. I'll take care of it."

In the following week Mac Sedaka became a famous
figure on Ronnie's block in Mill Basin. He walked her
youngest, Gary, in his baby carriage every day, all
around the neighborhood. Mac would stop at each
house he came to and ring the bell.

"Please be my daughter's friend," he said when an
irritated housewife came to the door, drying her hands
on a dish towel.

"We don't want any," she said, confused and looking
at Gary in the baby carriage. "What is it you want?"

"I want you to be my daughter's friend."

She peered at Mac's happy open countenance and
broke into laughter. "Aren't you the new people down
the block?"

"Yes. And this fine young man here is my daughter Ronnie's son. Ronnie's sort of shy, but she really wants to be sociable."

"Well, for heaven's sake, tell her I'll come by for a cup of coffee."

When Gary was a little older, he said to me, "Uncle Neil, Poppa would push me in my carriage and talk to everyone we passed. He has so many friends, and they became my friends, too."

Dara was growing like a weed. At six months she could say "Da-da," and by a year and a half she would strike up a conversation with strangers on the beach, saying, "My mother never feeds me." I couldn't wait to give Dara piano lessons. I used to sit her on my lap while I played the piano, taking her little finger and guiding it along the keys while I sang along. At Esther's hotel in Monticello, Dara would sit in the lobby and entertain people. At first Esther and Dara didn't get along. But after Leba and I took a trip, leaving Dara with Esther for several weeks, the two seemed inseparable. On Sundays, when we had to return to Brooklyn, Dara would cry and pull every trick in the book to remain with Esther. She usually pulled it off.

The only hint of vanished fame occurred when one of my old records occasionally played on the oldies radio station. There was once an article in a magazine entitled "Whatever happened to . . . ?" which included my name. And once in a while, I would meet people who asked, "How come we don't hear you on the radio any more? Neil Diamond is doing so well." Neil Diamond's parents lived in Brighton. He had a hit on the radio, and his career was blossoming. When his mother went to the Brighton Beach Baths, everyone made a fuss. I think this was more annoying to my mother than to me. I was getting to be very happy as an ordinary human being.

Screen Gems had started their own record label, and one day I decided to go to Don Kirshner with a new song called "Rainy Jane." Howie and I made a demo record that really sounded like a finished master, and Screen Gems released it with a minimum of hoopla or promotion. Although I only heard it twice in New York, I felt the old performing juices starting to flow.

I called an old friend of mine, Mike Borshetta, an independent promotions man in L.A., who I had worked with before, and he booked me on a radio station. Instead of the ordinary talk interview, I was to play and sing for an hour on live radio. It was an old programming concept given new life, and it came off very well.

After the show, the switchboard operator told me there was a call for me.

"Lawrence Welk," she said, "is on the line."

"Someone's got to be playing a joke," I told her. But when I got on the phone, I was amazed to discover it was indeed Lawrence Welk calling.

"Neil, you were wunnerful, just wunnerful. I really loved your performance. Don't ever let your singing and songwriting go to waste."

In gratitude, I sent him a number of my newest songs the next day. Nor did Lawrence Welk forget me. Years later he did a tribute to me on his show. I truly appreciated his support.

Unfortunately, "Rainy Jane" didn't get off the ground. A little later I gave the song to David Jones of The Monkees to record, and it immediately hit the charts. I was able to write hit songs for others, but Neil Sedaka the performer was totally washed up.

CHAPTER 17

CUTTING THE KOSHER CORD

On October 16, 1966, Leba gave birth to a son, Marc Charles Sedaka. This time the delivery was not so easy. My family and I waited for hours before Dr. Golliger came down to give us the good news. In contrast to Dara, Marc was a quiet and content baby. There were no tantrums or breath holding as there had been with Dara. He was happy to sit by himself with toys or blocks. Maybe it was because we fussed so much over the first child that with Marc we took things in stride, not standing over him and spoiling him. Dara and Marc were delighted with each other.

We hired a maid from Dominica named Mary Moses. She was good with children and a fabulous cook. I gained forty pounds because of her. Her mustard chicken and leg of lamb were out of this world.

Although I was happy raising my family, I felt I was neglecting part of my talent by not performing.

My business was being run as haphazardly as usual. I said to Leba, "The finances of the companies are completely out of control. Mom does the best she can, but she is not an accountant or bookkeeper. Things are written down on small scraps of paper and lost. We are still given this ridiculous allowance."

The situation got so tense I felt the whole family structure beginning to crumble around me. This made me very unhappy since I was basically a family man. My father became upset when he realized the extent of my misery. He said to me, "More friction, more quarrelling and disagreements all the time now, Neil. Something has to be done."

My friend Irving Hanna said to me one day, "Neil, look to your business affairs. Cut the strings."

Irv was right. My career was at a low ebb and now my marriage and my relationship with my mother were being affected. My financial situation was very shaky. There were too many questions unanswered.

Finally my anger boiled over.

"Leba," I told her one day, "I'm going to have a showdown with Mom."

She couldn't believe it. "What will your mother say?" The old fears resurfaced. She was afraid of the repercussions.

"My mind is made up," I said angrily. "It's time I got out of this ridiculous situation and we started running our own lives. I'm not a child. I'm a married man with a family. My God, Leba, we can't buy a roll of toilet paper without getting approval."

Leba had never seen me so upset. But she agreed that it had to be done. I tried to soften the blow all week, but it was too much for Mom when I told her I was taking charge of my life. She broke out crying, and I left my offices on Seventh Avenue completely shaken.

A while later the phone rang. It was Ronnie.

"Mom has taken an overdose of pills," she said. "I've just called for an ambulance."

I ran for the car and drove like a maniac with Irv and Leba. I found my mother lying on the bathroom floor.

Mom was unable to get up from the floor, and she refused to be taken to the hospital by ambulance. I took her in my car to Coney Island Hospital's emergency room where they pumped her stomach. It was horrible. I felt sick about it, too, but I couldn't let her change my mind. This was something it had taken me years to wake up to.

My mother and I were aloof for some time after the incident. This broke my heart. We had been so close. I finally called Fred Gershon to ask him for advice on my business and my career. He suggested a new accountant and a new tax lawyer, and he and his partner became my attorneys. Within a few weeks he began to put my affairs in order.

I vowed that if it was the last thing I ever did, I was to make a comeback.

CHAPTER 18

COMING BACK IS HARD TO DO

The children were growing up. Marc was now three, and Dara six and a half. When Dara had turned six I thought the time had come for her first piano lessons. Rather than hiring a teacher, I decided that with all the love between us, I could teach Dara myself. She was so musical that I thought it would be an easy task.

It was not. Because I was her father, she was not responsive to my criticism. Dara's ear was so good, she refused to learn to read the notes. She always asked me to play the piece first, then she would repeat it perfectly note by note, by ear. It was time to devise another method. Everyone in the family urged me to hire a music teacher.

I decided to try an unusual idea. One day I told Dara

that a Dr. Bergunka was coming to give her piano lessons. As the day of the lesson drew nearer I talked
about Dr. Bergunka with a stern look on my face.
"Bergunka is a very strict teacher," I told her. "He
won't take any nonsense. You must learn to read the
notes or else Dr. Bergunka will be very angry and hit
you over the hands with a very large ruler." Dara's eyes
widened and she began to think carefully about the
coming lesson.

The day of the piano lesson arrived. While Dara was
in her bedroom I put on a hat, a long coat, a pair of
glasses and sneaked out of the apartment. I looked like
an old menacing teacher from the film *The Seventh
Veil*. When I rang the front doorbell Dara came running to the door. "Who is it?" she said. Disguising my
voice I said, "It's Dr. Bergunka." Dara opened the door
slowly, and saw me dressed up in my disguise.

"Hello, are you Dara Sedaka? I am the piano teacher,
Dr. Bergunka," I said in a thick German accent. "We
have an appointment for a piano lesson."

Even though Dara knew it was her father, I could see
she was a bit frightened. The disguise, although not
very convincing, seemed to do the trick. We both
played along with the little game. She somehow was
more alert and serious about learning. She began to
take my criticism. When the lesson was over I said,
"Dara, I will see you next week. Don't forget to practice. I don't want to use my big ruler on your hands."
This game lasted for weeks, until Dara started telling
her school friends, "My mommy sleeps with Dr. Bergunka, my piano teacher."

* * *

We continued to spend part of the summer at Grandma Esther's hotel in Monticello, New York, with its indoor and outdoor swimming pools, a beautiful night club, tennis courts and magnificent grounds. It was also the closest hotel to the Monticello Raceway. Esther's slogan was "Small enough to know you. Big enough to serve you." Esther and her sister Irene were partners in this summer resort and worked fourteen to eighteen hours a day to prove the slogan. Leba and Barbara, her sister, often helped behind the desk. Even I pitched in for a time as a switchboard operator—until I was let go for listening in!

Then, one year, Esther took ill and was forced to sell the hotel. It came as a shock to all of us, especially Esther. The hotel was a way of life for her. She and Irv continued living in their home in Monticello, and Leba and I brought the family up there on the weekends. We loved that part of New York so much that Leba and I talked about getting a house around there, in the Catskill Mountains, and looked at some property when we were up there. Marc Shreibman, a friend of Leba's from high school who lived in Merriewold Park suggested we come up for a visit and look at the area.

The day we drove up there, Merriewold Park looked like a winter wonderland, the giant evergreens were covered with glistening snow. The area included hundreds of wooded acres and a majestic frozen lake. Marc later told us that deer, rabbit and muskrats roamed the grounds. The park was originally set up as an artist's colony. Leba and I loved it.

Marc suggested the cheapest way to go about purchasing a home was to buy a piece of land and build a small A-frame. The idea appealed to Leba. Merriewold was close enough to her parents for frequent visits, yet far enough from Monticello, which was very congested in the summer. This would be much more private and might be very good for my songwriting.

Marc introduced me to the Gonzaleses, who owned a tiny gingerbread house facing the golf course. The house had two small bedrooms, a small living room, dinette and kitchen. The location was perfect—not far from the entrance to the park, an important feature in a place where the roads in winter were sometimes made impenetrable with ice and snow. When I asked the Gonzaleses if their house was for sale, they said yes. They wanted $40,000.

The thought of building something new didn't appeal to me. I had limited funds, and I knew if Leba and Marc got together they'd come up with a structure à la Frank Lloyd Wright or Buckminster Fuller's geodesic dome. And I loved the feel of the Gonzales house—it somehow seemed right.

Leba fought me tooth and nail. She hated the house. I promised her I'd put work into it, really make it into a beautiful home. After much bickering, she agreed. When the Gonzaleses raised the price to $45,000, Leba had a fit. But we bought it anyway.

There was a committee at Merriewold who interviewed prospective homeowners. Merriewold in many ways was almost a private club, and the governing committee controlled the electricity. If they didn't vote to accept you in the club, you were left with no lights. Some of the other homeowners in Merriewold included George Abbott, Agnes de Mille, and Mary Rodgers

Guettel, the daughter of Richard Rodgers. They were not overjoyed about having a rock 'n' roller, especially one married to a Monticello girl. I thought I could almost read their prejudices in their faces—"Now our park will be overrun with all the Jews from town." Apparently, however, I had misread them—we were accepted.

After Leba and I moved in, our close friends Susan and Bruce Morrow were soon to follow, as well as Fred Gershon and his wife Myrna. Fred bought a funny little place we alternately called "Abe Lincoln's Log Cabin," "Gershon's Problem," and "Nolan's Delight." The Nolans had been the previous owners, before unloading it on the Gershons. The house had only one tiny bedroom, a kitchen, and a sleeping loft with a ladder. Fred, who had now given up his law practice to become president of the Robert Stigwood Organization, invited Robert for Thanksgiving weekend. He didn't really expect Stigwood to accept, as he knew Robert was going to Bermuda that weekend. To his shock, that Thursday Robert pulled up to the tiny cabin in his limousine.

"Fred," he said, "what a cute gatekeeper's house. But where is the main house? Where do you live?"

Fred explained that this was not only the main one, but the only one. Robert Stigwood had to sleep in the loft.

Leba began to help with the management of my career—what little was left of it in the late sixties. She had a natural talent for business, coupled with her experience at her mother's hotel. Soon there was an offer to perform in Australia, and I was able to try out new material there, put together a new act, and record on Festival Records. My "Star-Crossed Lovers" went to number 1 in Australia. Except for an occasional one-nighter in the Catskills, Australia was about the only action I was to see in the late sixties.

In 1970 Don Kirshner decided to start his own label, which he planned to have distributed by RCA. I wanted a career in America again desperately, and this seemed like a golden opportunity. I approached Don about a chance to record a new LP, and he gave me the go-ahead.

Howie Greenfield and I wrote with a vengeance. Howie outdid himself. The collection was brilliant, including such songs as "Superbird," "Cardboard California," "Sing Me," and "Gone with the Morning." It was high quality pop that could have come from a smash musical on Broadway.

At the time Howie and I were finishing our songs, my old girlfriend Carole King released her LP, *Tapestry*, an album inspired by James Taylor, one of the people she hung out with. His *Sweet Baby James* was at the top of the charts. After songwriting for several years, Carole had attempted performing with bands several times unsuccessfully before recording *Tapestry*. I heard a couple of cuts on the air, and they took my breath away. I ran out to buy the LP—as did 14 million other people—and played it constantly. In many ways the melodic approach, the piano fills, the vocal phrasing were similar to my own.

"Of course they are," Howie told me. "Carole was

one of your biggest fans back in the fifties. I almost feel
as if I'm listening to your songs."

Carole had been very clever, though. She had incorporated a small group of rock musicians as an integral
part of her sound, and the music seemed fresh, new and
alive.

I decided that my new collection should be treated
the same way, and I vowed I would be just as successful as Carole. But when I told Donnie how I
wanted the new LP to be recorded, he disagreed.

"Neil, you have a classical piano background. You
should have a large, lush-sounding orchestra to show
off your talents."

My instincts disagreed, but I went along with him. I
liked the arranger Lee Holdridge though—the arrangements he made were stunning, and some of the pieces
almost sounded symphonic. My vocals and piano playing almost took a second seat. It was definitely a show-
case for the songs and Lee Holdridge.

An orchestra was hired by Lee for the recording. I
entitled the collection *Emergence*, which seemed very
apropos as this was my first recording in a long time.
Even though the mixes did not sound particularly Top
40ish, there was a certain magic in the record, a time-
less feeling about it. Everyone told me the songs were
brilliant.

When it was released in 1970, I decided to take to the
road. RCA was not enthusiastic, so I paid for everything myself. I should have realized at that time that
when your record company is not excited about your
record and does not spend time or money on it, the
record is practically dead in its tracks.

In an effort to promote *Emergence*, I was booked by my agent, Dick Fox, at the Bitter End in New York. Don Kirshner was there, as well as several other people from the record industry. Carol Sager called me up a day before the show to offer me advice.

"Neil," she said, "you've got to look laid back, part of the scene." She dyed a T-shirt for me and shrunk a pair of faded jeans to give me a more "in" look. The backup band consisted of a bass, drums and guitar, and Barbara Goldberg, an old high school friend, sang the backgrounds. I planned the set in Merriewold, and included oldies as well as the new material. The continuity had to be right. I was terrified that the act wouldn't go over. Except for Australia, I hadn't been onstage in a long time. To add to my tension, this was New York City, with the most sophisticated and critical audience in the world.

My anxiety disappeared as soon as I walked out on the stage opening night. The room only sat a hundred or so. I felt as if I were entertaining people in my living room, in Brooklyn. I was totally relaxed and confident. The fast pacing and the mixture of old and new brought the crowd to its feet. I felt a sudden charge, an audience electricity I hadn't felt in years.

When the *Record World* review came out, it reported SEDAKA A SMASH AT THE BITTER END. Leba had it blown up for me and framed. The encouragement I'd received from the crowds at the Bitter End gave me hope that similar performances in clubs in other cities would stir up record sales of *Emergence*.

In Chicago I played a small club called the Quiet Night. Opening night was on the lukewarm side. The

place was not packed and most of the audience consisted of curiosity seekers who came to hear the old
Neil Sedaka do "Calendar Girl" and "Breaking Up."
The next morning, after running out in a wicked Chicago snowstorm to buy the local paper, I discovered the
review was devastating. It was written by a rock critic
who only liked Dylan and underground acts. He tore
me to shreds and advised that I give up any attempt at a
comeback. "Sedaka had his days from '59 to '62. There
is no way he'll ever be contemporary again. The songs
are lightweight, the singing passé." He especially dis-
liked Howie's lyrics. I was hurt, but not being the type
that's easily discouraged, I continued on to Denver,
where I played at a club called Marvelous Marv's. My
engagement followed that of a new hot singer named
Linda Ronstadt. They were still talking about her
when I opened.

Opening night the house was packed. The room was
a sea of cowboy hats and boots, and their response to
me was overwhelming. Either I was getting better, or
Denver was more agreeable to me. The reviewers liked
my voice and melodies, but again they knocked
Howie's lyrics.

Howie was one of the best lyricists in the business.
His lyrics were very slick and polished, like tiny, compact novels, self-contained dramas. I called Howie the
King of the Cover Records. People still love to record
his songs. His lyrics work particularly well in Vegas
cabarets and night clubs with the over-thirty crowd.

But by 1970 lyrics had changed as radically as melodies. Composers like James Taylor, Paul Simon and
Cat Stevens were painting images. Their words were

more elusive, more poetic. They created a mood rather than telling a story.

I called Leba every night from the road to report how the act was going. *Emergence* was not receiving any air time. It just didn't fit the tastes of the current rock audience, who were listening to groups like The Stones, Crosby, Stills, Nash, and Young, Deep Purple, and Led Zeppelin. When Howie and I played *Emergence* for our friends, the teenagers and college students didn't like it—but our older friends loved it. Mary Rodgers Guettel thought *Emergence* was wonderful. "I want you to meet my father," she said. "I think he'd love this. Let me set up an appointment." I readily agreed. Richard Rodgers was the greatest musical composer of his era. I had listened to his marvelous pop songs and show tunes all my life; I used to sing his songs with my band in the Catskills.

I introduced myself to Richard Rodgers at his beautiful office on Madison Avenue. He told me that he had listened to *Emergence* and thought it was wonderful.

"Would you mind playing for me a little?" he asked.

I sat at the piano and played some new songs I was writing. After a few songs he interrupted me.

"Come away from the piano, Neil," he said. "That's too easy for you. You should write a show. Your songs would be great on the musical stage."

I was very flattered, but I had vowed to make it to the top again as a rock 'n' roll star.

CHAPTER 19
OUR LAST
SONG
TOGETHER

While Leba and I were in New York we went to see
Diana Ross at the Empire Room at the Waldorf Astoria
for her first solo appearance since the breakup of The
Supremes. She gave a spectacular performance and invited us up to her suite afterwards, where we were introduced to Tom Jones, who had just become a national
phenomenon.

"Neil, we've met before," he told me. "Don't you remember? At Arthur?" Arthur was the popular disco in
New York started by Sybil Burton, Richard Burton's
ex-wife. Tom was opening at the Copacabana the following evening. "Why don't you come to my show tomorrow night," he suggested. "I'm going to be singing
your song, 'Puppet Man'. I'd love to have you hear it.
Call my manager, Gordon Mills, and he'll arrange it."

But when I called Gordon, he said, "Neil, it's a mad-house at the Copa. Your best bet is to meet us at the Hotel 14 next door to the Copa and come down with Tom."

The following evening we met Tom at the Hotel 14, where the Copa kept a suite for the headliners. An elevator took us down to the kitchen at the Copa. We stepped off the elevator and into bedlam. Teenagers, middle-aged couples and female fans of all ages overwhelmed us, tearing at our clothes. Security guards had to carry Tom through to the stage. Leba and I remained in the back, ready to make a quick getaway if necessary. The crowd was at a fever pitch, and as the show opened, women began screaming and throwing their undergarments and room keys onto the stage. One woman was half naked. It was incredible. After a few songs, we realized there was no way we could hear Tom over the screaming, and Leba and I decided we had had enough. I never did get to see him do "Puppet Man."

Emergence turned out to be a commercial failure. It did, however, have a cult following, and it proved to a number of people that Neil Sedaka was still a contender. I was disappointed but not discouraged. If I wanted to rise to the top, though, I realized I had to change my writing style. And that meant a new lyricist. After twenty years of writing together, I had no idea how to break this to Howie. Surprisingly, Howie too, felt it was time for a change. He decided to move to L.A. with his longtime friend Tonr Damon.

We wrote two songs before he left. "Our Last Song

Together" incorporated many titles of songs we had done in the past. It was poignant and beautiful:

> Days of devils, kings and clowns,
> Angel songs and birthday tunes,
> Silly rhymes, monkey shines,
> Pictures on a stage.
> Round and round the records go,
> Time to turn the page.
>
> The tra-la days are over.
> Those days of me and you.
> Now we know that breaking up
> Is really hard to do.

When it was finished I sang it in the den at Seacoast Terrace. Leba, Tony, Howie and I wept.

The other song, ironically, was "Love Will Keep Us Together."

The record industry is extremely fickle. It's trendy, cliquish, and full of phonies. When you're on top, you're surrounded by backslappers and yes men. You're a hero and everyone wants to be around you. But when you're down, you're yesterday's news. The phone doesn't ring. You're not invited to the "A" parties. In the record business you can go from a star to a has-been within six months. The question is constantly, "What have you done lately?" The trends change rapidly, and if you can't keep up with them, you're left behind.

In 1970 I couldn't get arrested. No record company would touch me. I was a ghost from the past, an oldies

act, nostalgia trivia. Many of the oldies shows called
me, but I couldn't bring myself to do them. I thought
they were very sad—performers who had hits years
ago, who now had jobs as salesmen or insurance bro-
kers, brought back to sing their old hits. They were
relics who couldn't keep up with the musical times. I
couldn't see myself still singing "Happy Birthday
Sweet Sixteen" at age thirty-one.

I began seaching frantically for a new lyricist. One
day I met lyricist Phil Cody at Kirshner's, who had recently put out an album of his own. Taking a copy
home with me, I carefully followed the lyrics on the
liner notes. They were just what I had been looking for,
poetic and youthful, full of images, pictures, and
moods.

Phil had just broken off with his writing partner. I
went into his office the next day and asked him if he
wanted to collaborate on some songs with me. Phil was
quiet and painfully shy, but I had taken to him immediately.

He looked at me strangely, as if to say, "Is this old
man kidding?" But after a moment's hesitation, he said,
"Why not?"

There seemed to be magic between Phil and I from
the moment we began. His lyrics were fluid, flexible
and very musical, and his word choice and rhymes
were not as predictable as Howie's. Best of all, he didn't
limit my melodies. I could write freely, with extra beats
and extended bars. I felt as if I had been let out of a
cage, as if a whole new world of melody was open to me.

Phil and I wrote five songs in the first week, including "Baby, Don't Let It Mess Your Mind," "Home,"

and "Trying to Say Goodbye." We were both excited with our work.

"I've never written with anyone with so much drive and enthusiasm," he told me. "The joy you give off is contagious."

Phil and I wrote Monday through Friday in the office, and on weekends in Merriewold Park. When the lyrics were done, Phil would disappear to the basement to play pool or dabble on the piano. He found it painful to talk or mingle with people. He was a true artist and writer, living his life primarily through his work. When we weren't working, he'd write by himself, playing his latest creations for me later. He had a lovely voice, and accompanied himself on piano or guitar. He also had the amazing ability to sit at the piano and improvise a song off the top of his head. Most of the time it sounded like a finished, beautiful melody, as if he'd worked on it for hours. At parties Phil would sit and entertain everyone.

Dick Fox, my agent at the William Morris Agency, heard the new Cody-Sedaka songs, and thought they were highly commercial. One day we sat around for hours in his office, discussing my career and what directions to take, when he came up with an idea: "Why not attempt a comeback in England?"

"Why England?" I asked.

"America watches England very closely. There are only two major radio stations, the BBC I and II. If you can crack them, you're on the air all over England, Scotland and Ireland. And the English fans are faithful. They remember you from 1961. There is a genuine regard for American entertainers—Roy Orbison, Gene

Pitney and Del Shannon are touring there now. Why not begin singing your old hits there and slowly incorporate your new material? America is a tough nut to crack. There are too many stations, and they have too many preconceived ideas about Neil Sedaka."

The British seemed to be much more aware of the roots of rock 'n' roll, and they knew that I was one of the forerunners, one of the originators. The Beatles and other such groups were inspired by people like Carole King, Chuck Berry, Little Richard and myself.

When an offer came for a cabaret act in northern England from British promoter Henry Sellers, Leba and I decided to take it.

The clubs turned out be real "holes." The first was a depressing beer joint in Liverpool catering to a rowdy clientele. I sang mostly old material, while the audience drank and talked through the act. After the show I was seized by depression. What was I trying to do? Perhaps I was grasping at straws, and I would never achieve stardom again. After all, no one from the fifties and early sixties had ever made a comeback before.

On opening night in Manchester, there were only twenty people in the audience. My act followed a stripper. The acoustics were deplorable. Every time I tried to sing something other than my old hits, people began to talk and clink their beer glasses. Leba and I were beginning to think that England was a big mistake. I remember once in Stockton, England, I came back to my tiny hotel room after a miserable gig. It might have been suicidally depressing had it not been for the blessing of my family, who were playing and laughing in the dingy room when I returned. Leba was showing

Marc how to play with Lego—the British version of the erector set. When I collapsed into a comalike sleep, Marc sat up, watching me for hours.

There was an offer to do a one-nighter at the Albert Hall in London. I hired a drummer, a bassist, and a cellist as my instrumental backup, and I made up a set comprised of half old hits and half new material.

The Albert Hall is a menacing edifice. At the sound check, I was scared to death. The acoustics were horrible. Before the show I went out and downed three gin martinis, one after another.

When I walked out on the stage that night and began to sing, the hall was only half full. But with each old hit the applause grew stronger. When I reached the section of new songs, I took a deep breath and plunged on, singing "Trying to Say Goodbye" and "Don't Let It Mess Your Mind." You could hear a pin drop. After more than an hour I did "Solitaire." I wondered if the people had all left; the silence was deafening. The song seemed to go on forever. I finally reached the last lines:

> Solitaire, the only game in town
> And every road that takes him takes him
>   down.
> While life goes on around him
>   everywhere
> He's playing solitaire.

I stopped. All of a sudden the silence broke. There was thunderous applause. They were stamping their feet and cheering. I stood up in shock. I walked off as the audience yelled "Bravo." They begged for an encore.

The press came running back to my dressing room after the concert. They were falling all over me—all kinds of accolades and compliments. I had seen this sort of thing in the movies, but now it was happening to me. The next day the papers were filled with great reviews. But I still had a long way to go. I had worked very hard to get to this point. I wasn't going to let it stop now. The English public was behind me. From this concert on, my career slowly began to turn. The next couple of years it was to go beyond my wildest dreams.

With Barbra Streisand and Jon Peters

With Elton John—
just kidding!

With Frankie Valli, Dinah Shore and Tony Orlando

With the ageless Dick Clark
(Peter C. Borsari)

With Bette Midler
during one of
my TV specials

With Andy Gibb, Dara Sedaka, and The Captain and Tenille
during another Sedaka television special

With Maurice Gibb
beside the jet plane
we bought together

With Mike Douglas, Fred Astaire and Gene Kelly during the week I co-hosted
the *Mike Douglas Show* (*Group W Productions, photographer: Michael Leshnov*)

The Sedakas in 1981

With McLean Stevenson on *The Tonight Show*
(Courtesy NBC)

With Freddie Gershon

With my sister Ronnie

The Nordenels were reunited at a party celebrating my twenty-fifth year as a songwriter. Left to right: Howard Tischler, me, Leba, Dave Bass, Esther Strassberg (Leba's mother) and Norman Spizz

With Leba and Princess Anne at a Royal Charity Gala concert in 1979

The Sedakas with Parker Stevenson and Alexandra Spadafora
in Rio de Janeiro during Carnival, 1982

CHAPTER 20
ROCK 'N' ROLL LAZARUS

As a result of the Albert Hall concert, the Talk of the Town in London booked me for a three week run. The Talk of the Town is a classy club that caters to both the tourist crowd and to local regulars. It was quite a difference from the Wooky Hollow, and I began to revise the act accordingly. The first rule in night club performing is to know the type of crowd you're playing for, and try to please them. A performer can't try to educate them too much or assume they're stupid. He always has to hold himself a little above them—be humble, but believe in himself at the same time. If it was not a particularly receptive audience, I had discovered it was best to lay back and let them come to me. Most of all I had to look confident and make them think they're lucky to be there.

For the Talk of the Town I decided to include some
numbers where I could get away from the piano and
move around the stage. Besides my own songs, I included big band arrangements of Cat Stevens's "Father
and Son," "I Feel the Earth Move" by Carole King,
and Johnny Nash's "I Can See Clearly Now." This se-
lection would provide the act with peaks and valleys. A
good performer starts slowly and gradually builds the
intensity—if he starts too strong, there's nowhere to go.
After moving the audience to tears with an emotional
piece, you have to follow with a spirited song that will
rouse them to their feet. A performance, I knew, is like
a love affair—if the performer is lucky. And good. But
he has to be "up" for it. As I learned the hard way, it
takes two to tango.

Often I know as soon as I set foot on a stage whether
it's going to be a good audience or not. An audience
definitely has vibrations. If the majority of the audience
is there to have a good time, they'll sway the entire
room. If they seem determined not to have a good time,
the performance can miss. It is a challenge, a battle
of wits. Can I win them? Can I make them love me?

The Talk of the Town was a sell-out, and the owners
extended my stay to five weeks. After my last show I
ran off the stage to my dressing room screaming, "A triumph, it was a triumph." I flung open my dressing
room door, and there sat Englebert Humperdinck,
dressed to the nines. I was completely taken aback.

"Yes, it was a triumph," he smiled.

I was embarrassed, to say the least. But I did think it
a bit presumptuous of him to go to my dressing room
without my permission. I was elated that he thought it

was a triumph, but it did take away from my private moment.

While working in England I had a visit from Harvey Listberg, who was a personal manager for many British acts. I had first met him in New York at Don Kirshner's office, when he had selected a song of mine called "Amarillo" for one of his singers, Tony Christie. "Amarillo" had become an international hit, although it never sold well in the U.S. He now told me of a new group he had founded, Hotlegs (who later became known as 10 cc). They had a studio in Stockport, outside of Manchester, and Harvey wanted me to record two or three of my new songs with them. He raved on about them, and since I had faith in his judgment, I took the trip to their Strawberry Studios. The were recording when I arrived. I was amazed—they had an extraordinary sound and were obviously very talented. The group was then made up of Graham Gouldman on bass, Eric Stewart and Lol Creme on guitar, and Kevin Godley on drums. They all sang extremely well. I was so impressed I wound up recording an entire album at Strawberry Studios, singing the lead vocals and playing piano.

I found it was a real luxury to go into a studio and record without looking at a clock. It was very different from East Twenty-fourth Street in New York, the RCA Studios. At Strawberry we spent hours, day and night, recording my songs, taking occasional breaks and going out for Chinese food. I loved it. This was the way I should've always recorded. We were having fun and making good music at the same time.

During the time I was recording with 10 cc in Stockport, Leba and I were having drinks in the lobby of our hotel when a bizarrely dressed group of people came in. "That's David Bowie and his group," whispered an English girl behind me.

I asked Leba, "Who's David Bowie?"

"I'm not sure exactly, but I've heard his name in the United States. They say he's an up-and-coming rock musician."

Bowie was fascinating—a tall, willowy, well-built man, with fine, beautiful facial features, almost pretty enough to be a woman. I had not heard his records yet as he hadn't been around very long.

I couldn't help staring at him across the room. After a while he looked at me and smiled. Walking over to me he said, "Hello—aren't you Neil Sedaka?"

"Yes," I replied.

"I've been a great fan of yours for a long time. My name is David Bowie."

"Yes, I've read about you," I lied.

"I've heard that you're recording with 10 cc at Strawberry Studios," he said. "Would you mind if I came up and sat in for a while? I would love to have a chance to hear you record. In fact, if you'd like, I would be glad to play guitar on one or two cuts." He was very friendly, and with his personality and looks, he could charm anyone.

"Thank you very much. I appreciate your offer, but I'm afraid the session is closed. I never allow visitors when I am recording." We talked for a few minutes and he told us about closing down Mr. Fish, a trendy men's apparel store. Bowie was very much into a bisexual look, occasionally wearing full dresses with makeup.

"Customers refused to shop there," Bowie said half-jokingly, "because of my association with the store."

As he walked away, Leba said, "I think you made a mistake. You should have accepted his offer to play on your album. I know you become self-conscious, but they all say he'll become a superstar. It would have been a feather in your cap to have had him play.'"

Leba was right. Six months later, with the release of his *Ziggy Stardust* album, David Bowie became a worldwide celebrity with a powerful cult following. He is a true innovator with his songs as well as his unusual costumes and the lighting effects at his concerts. Bowie is a genius at special stage effects, and became one of the first to effectively use pantomime, makeup and multicolored hairstyles to establish a special kind of image.

The recording was finished in three weeks. The cost, $5,000, was almost nothing. An unheard-of total. The LP included "Music Takes Me," "Express Yourself," "Better Days," "Dimbo Man," and "Solitaire," which we also used as the album title. Eric Stewart and I did the mixing, and then we went to Apple Records to cut the master. When we were finished I went directly to the airport with the record to return to the U.S. But in the taxi, I realized that something was bothering me. "Leba," I said, "I want to cancel our flight and recut the master record. I don't think it has enough highs, and it lacks midrange. There's not enough clarity. It's got to be improved." Leba agreed and we directed the taxi back to Apple Records, where at last it was remixed to my satisfaction.

In New York the next day, tired and jet-lagged, I

tracked down Donnie Kirshner. When I played him the master, he was a bit reserved at first, uncertain whether this was the right direction for me. I had such faith in the album I said, "I'd be willing to buy it from you and put it out myself." I think at that point Donnie decided he loved it. The record did not do well in America, but England picked up on it.

In fact, England was beginning to seem to me to be an altogether more hospitable climate and I began to spend time there. "What about taking a flat in London and living there several months a year?" Leba suggested. It would mean giving up Brooklyn and taking the kids out of public school, uprooting ourselves to start a new life. But my career was beginning to flourish in England, and there was nothing for me in America. It was a scary decision, but we decided to do it.

We packed up all our belongings, the two children, and our housekeeper, Mary Moses, and registered at the Carlton Towers Hotel in London while we proceeded to look for an apartment. A representative of RCA Victor called with good news: "The *Solitaire* LP is doing very well, and we're releasing 'Beautiful You' as a single." I thought "Beautiful You" was a wonderful choice, very funky and bluesy. This was a song that could reach a much younger audience.

But just as I thought I was breaking away from my old 1950s image, there was a sudden turn of events. A number of old hit records reissued in 1972 were selling very well, and an RCA executive decided to rerelease my original "Oh, Carol." History was about to repeat itself. The record that had started my career in 1959 was about to launch my comeback twelve years later.

The original 45 of "Oh, Carol" immediately climbed the charts in Britain—at the same time as "Beautiful You" and the *Solitaire* album were flying out of the stores. Kids who had never heard of Neil Sedaka before were singing "Oh, Carol," and reviewers were calling me a rock 'n' roll Lazarus, rising from the dead. RCA began repackaging all my big hits. "Your determination and drive are paying off," Leba said.

With a comeback all but guaranteed, Leba and I moved the family to a beautiful old flat on Park Street, behind the Dorchester Hotel in Mayfair. The rent was high, but it was a huge nine-room apartment.

"Oh, Carol" reached number 19 on the English charts, and "Beautiful You" climbed as high as the 30s. As a result, *Top of the Pops*, the popular British teenage TV show, asked me on the show to do "Oh, Carol." I was a bit disappointed that it wasn't "Beautiful You," but I knew my new LP was still doing well. *Solitaire* started to get a lot of attention as well.

Leba continued to call all the record people, agents and promoters, stirring up publicity for me, and I toured all over the country. One club I particularly liked was Batley, owned by James and Betty Corrigan. It was the nicest of the northern clubs, and Batley's hired only the biggest names. Derek Smith, the manager, was kind enough to comment, after watching my rehearsal from the wings, "Neil, you're going to bring down the house tonight. This is only the start. You should be in Vegas or Lincoln Center." I played Batley many times, and the Corrigans invited me to stay in their home, treating me as part of the family.

Leba negotiated a contract for me with Polydor

Records, and I began writing a new collection of songs for my first LP with them. During this time I was commuting back and forth to New York, spending six months in Merriewold Park and six months in London. Merriewold, I had come to realize, was a wonderful place to create. My piano was situated in front of a large picture window with a magnificent view of the woods. Phil Cody and I finished our collection there, and once again I recorded the songs at Strawberry Studios with 10 cc. They had become a monstrous success in Europe in the last year.

The recording was a labor of love. I entitled the album *The Tra-la Days Are Over*. The cover had a vintage 1958 picture of me beside a current one. This was the album that finally shattered my old image and restored me to a place in contemporary music. The songs included "Little Brother," "Standing on the Inside," "Alone at Last," "Caribbean Rainbow," "Let Daddy Know," "Suspicion," "Love Will Keep Us Together," "Other Side of Me," "Rock 'n' Roll Wedding Day," "For Peace and Love," and "Our Last Song Together." Perhaps this was the album that would catch on in America. I hoped so.

CHAPTER 21
MAURICE GIBB

Maurice Gibb of The Bee Gees rang me at our flat in London.

"Listen," he said, "I've heard all about you, and I understand you live right around the corner. Why don't we get together for a drink?"

"I'd love to," I replied. "How about the Inn on the Park?"

I found Maurice Gibb an absolutely delightful person, bright, witty, and a tremendous musician. Maurice was married to Lulu at the time, the talented singer from Scotland. They were headed for divorce. Maurice and I would have Scotch and Cokes at the Saddle Room, a disco adjacent to the Inn on the Park, and each of us would pour out his frustrations and fears on each other's shoulders. This was a cold period for The Bee

Gees, and Maurice often accompanied me to my night club performances.

When The Bee Gees came to New York sometime later for a concert at Avery Fisher Hall, Maurice gave me a call and offered us tickets. Leba and I invited Fred and Myrna Gershon to join us. The concert was terrific. The Bee Gees had a beautiful string section and Robin Gibb's voice was in top form.

After the concert Leba and I returned with them to their hotel room at the City Squire on Seventh Avenue. Their father was there as well as their younger brother Andy, who was about twelve years old at the time. We spent a couple of hours singing together while Barry played guitar, harmonizing The Bee Gee's favorite songs, including my "Breaking Up Is Hard to Do" and "Happy Birthday Sweet Sixteen."

Maurice and I continued to keep in touch, and one day when I was working at the Talk of the Town he called unexpectedly, inviting me to go dancing at Tramps with Lulu and some friends. Lulu had bestselling records and her own TV show. She was full of personality and energy. The Bee Gees, however, had hit their all-time low, with very little happening in terms of record sales or concert tours.

The Gibbs owned a beautiful house in Hampstead, and Maurice, who had driven his Continental Bentley convertible to Tramps, had been drinking heavily. I was worried about his trip back home as we walked out.

"Maurice, are you sure you can drive home?" I asked.

Lulu maneuvered him home that night.

Weeks later, over drinks one night at the Saddle Room, Maurice told me it seemed like his marriage was ending.

"Maurice, you can depend on me whenever you need a shoulder to cry on." And Maurice needed a big pair of shoulders all the time. We spent hours together getting drunk. I knew he was in pain. He would often try to talk his way through his problems as we each downed drink after drink. One night, however, I really overdid the drinking—I must have had ten Scotch and Cokes. This time Maurice and Anthony Brown, a friend of his, had to carry *me* home.

"Neil, you're absolutely paralytic," Maurice laughed hysterically.

The next day I was sick as a dog. Maurice looked in on me, and we sat and listened to music. Then he gave me the news. "I'm getting a divorce."

"I'm sorry, Maurice. I really am. But I have to agree that it's the best thing."

Also, I could no longer sustain those all-night drinking sessions, much as I adored him.

It took some time, however, for Maurice to get Lulu completely out of his system. One night after the divorce I got a frantic phone call from him.

"Neil, Lulu has been in a terrible car accident. Oh, God, help me."

I drove like a maniac to his house only to find he was confused and having mild hallucinations.

Several years later Maurice went on the wagon, married a beautiful, charming girl, Yvonne, and The Bee

Gees went through one of the greatest comebacks of all time. Sensitive and talented in the extreme, Maurice is a man with the courage and will power to pull himself through.

CHAPTER 22
COMING OF AGE IN LONDON

It was during a Bee Gees concert in London that I first met Elton John. I was a tremendous fan of his and we have a few things in common—both of us are pianists and composers and have an abundance of energy and stamina. When Elton made his first major appearance in America, at Carnegie Hall, I was very flattered to hear from his record company that Elton had called and specifically asked that I be invited to attend the performance. I took along my daughter Dara, who adored it, especially "Crocodile Rock."

Back in London, when *The Tra-la Days Are Over* was released by Polydor, I received a call out of the blue from Elton. "I've heard about your new album, Neil. I just want to wish you all the success in England. You know what they're saying on the street about you—you're better than Carole King. You're the next American superstar. I'd love to come down to talk with you at your flat."

"Elton, I'd be so flattered."

He agreed to come down that afternoon. I didn't tell the family—I wanted it to be a surprise. Marc, who was only seven, had Elton John posters on every wall of his room.

When the doorbell rang, I yelled out to him, "Marc, would you see who it is?" When he opened the door, he almost keeled over. There, his hair streaked in several colors, wearing a funny jacket and green shoes, stood the greatest rock star in the world.

That afternoon I played some songs from my new LP for Elton, and he was very impressed. Then he sat down and played a few new songs he was writing with Bernie Taupin, including "Candle in the Wind" and "Don't Let the Sun Go Down on Me." I was spellbound. There were only a handful of people in the world who could do that. Elton seems down to earth, with a quiet, unassuming manner. But he is also a perfectionist. Everything he undertakes, he does well—including pinball, at which he truly is the wizard.

Elton invited me to Linda and Paul McCartney's party after one of their concerts. When I was introduced to Paul he started to sing "That's When the Music Takes Me," one of my songs. He was poised and sharp as a tack, and never at a loss for words—a very entertaining person. Rod Stewart was there, as well. In London I was surrounded by rock royalty and made to feel I was one of them.

Back in the United States, however, my situation had

not changed. I was just a ghost from the past. No appearances, no air play, no sales.

Don Kirshner made a deal with Mike Curb, a young record producer from L.A., who later became lieutenant governor of California. He had an executive position with MGM and owned his own label. He and his sister Carol, who together were in charge of their division, agreed to release a single record on MGM from the *Tra-la* LP in England—"Standing on the Inside." I heard the test pressing in New York and it sounded great. When the record was released, Leba and I took off for a well-deserved vacation at La Costa, a health spa in San Diego. I weighed about 170 lbs., and at five feet six, that's thirty-five pounds too much.

In L.A., I decided to drop in on the Curbs at MGM records to check on "Standing on the Inside." When Leba and I arrived at MGM the receptionist made us wait a long time in the reception room. Finally Carol Curb came out to see us.

"Hello," I said, "I'm Neil Sedaka and this is my wife Leba. We just dropped in to see how my record is doing."

Carol Curb gave me a blank look, and said "Neil who? What record?"

She wasn't even aware of the release. My record was just one of a bunch that were lying in a pile on the floor. I was livid. Talking to her was like talking to a wall. Leba and I got up and left.

On the drive back to La Costa I was steaming. I couldn't believe I was having all this success in England and nothing in America. About halfway through the trip I said, "Leba, I'm going to record in

L.A. Perhaps that will do it. I'm not familiar with the recording scene in California, but by God I'm going to find out about it."

Phil Cody and I decided to write a new collection of songs for the L.A. recording. Our best work still came out of Merriewold Park. Usually, I wrote a melody first and then Phil put the lyrics to it. The week we started writing, I had no melodies prepared. I began playing accompaniment on the piano while I searched vocally for the melody. Suddenly the first melodic lines of a song popped out almost by accident. Phil raised his eyebrows, as if to say, "Where did that come from?"

The mind gets into a certain state of creativity where there are no inhibitions. Being a performer, I love to write with someone—the feedback, the reaction, is important, and Phil is a great sounding board. It was a challenge seeing if I could move him emotionally. The creative juices were flowing and nothing else mattered except finishing the song. My fingers moved along the keys as if the melody was coming from a power beyond.

Songwriting has always frightened me. I feel like I'm a surgeon performing an operation without any formal knowledge or training. The patient can die at any moment. The more you do it, the easier it becomes, but the anxiety is always there. And it gets harder to please yourself each time.

At last the melody was finished. Phil came up with the title—"Laughter in the Rain." His lyrics were beautiful—laughing when the chips are down, during the continuous see-saw of ups and downs.

We wrote three songs that weekend. After Phil left

I continued to play "Laughter in the Rain." I called him hours later at his home to say how excited I was about it. After years of writing I knew we had something special.

When I arrived in L.A. for the recording, I checked into the Beverly Hills Hotel. The people behind the desk practically ignored me, and I stood there a long while. In L.A. you had to have a name—especially at the Beverly Hills Hotel. They finally gave me a small, depressing room. After unpacking, I went for a drink at the Polo Lounge. Asked if I had a reservation, I replied, "No."

"Then you'll have to sit at the bar," said the maître d'.

At last I was furious. Someday *I'm* going to be someone again, I said to myself.

That night I had a nightmare. I dreamed I was in a recording studio ready for a take and I had laryngitis. Nothing came out. The musicians all stared and laughed, and the engineer asked me to leave.

When I awoke it was a fresh, sunny L.A. morning. Palm trees waved outside the window. I ordered breakfast from room service. At last I was ready. I rented a car and drove to Clover Studios.

Clover Studios was an old, rickety building with a tiny entrance. When I asked for Robert Appere, the engineer, I was taken to a very slight, pale boy of about twenty-five. He looked undernourished and ill. Robert greeted me with a devilish smile. But despite his emaciated and boyish appearance, he seemed supremely confident. He spoke articulately in a quick, slightly nervous fashion. I knew immediately that I liked him.

I recorded the lead vocal and the piano parts for the new songs that night, and afterwards Robert had me listen to the sound. It certainly was different from RCA in New York or Strawberry in England—rougher, looser, not as compact as I was accustomed to. I didn't know if I liked it or not. We played my previous LPs, and in comparison, they sounded thinner, tinnier. The voice quality had no bottom, no balls. I began to like this L.A. sound.

The next day the musicians straggled in—two guitars, drums and bass. We rehearsed the first few times and put them down on the tape. It was bad. When the musicians walked out for a break, I didn't have to say anything to Robert—he sensed my disappointment automatically.

"They're not great musicians," he said. "The good musicians won't come until they're sure the material is up to their standards." These L.A. session men were stars in their own right.

"The word will get around fast," Robert said.

It did. The next day, Russ Kunkel on drums, Leeland Sklar on bass, and Danny Kooch and Dean Parks on guitars all came in. They had played on some of the biggest hit records. Now the songs started to come alive. I guess my excitement was contagious. The musicians had never seen a performer play the piano and sing simultaneously during a recording session before. Robert had had a special piano top built so that the sound of the piano would not leak into my vocal mike.

We rehearsed and recorded three songs in a row. We could all sense the excitement. "A Little Lovin"

sounded like an old rock 'n' roller, but modern and
raunchy. "The Way I Am" sounded like an Edgar
Winter tune, and "For the Good of the Cause" received
a funky gospel treatment. The best singers in town
came down—Abigail Haness, Brian and Brenda Russell, William Smith, and Donny Gerard. "The word's
all over Hollywood," Robert said, "Neil Sedaka's back
with some great tunes."

"Laughter in the Rain" was the next song to be recorded. I played it on the piano first to familiarize everyone. The musicians went wild over it. Robert said,
"Now watch them play their asses off."

Robert hired the great David Foster to play keyboards, as well as Jim Horn, a marvelous sax player.
Chuck Findlay came down with a first-rate brass section. The only person I hired was the string arranger
Artie Butler, and old friend from New York. Robert
had to put a sign on the front door—"No Visitors"—to
keep people out. The record was magic.

We decided to call the album *Laughter in the Rain*.
It was released by Polydor in England, and the LP
went high on the charts. The single of "Laughter"
topped out at number 14.

As a result of my new album I was booked at the
most important concert of my career—a show at Royal
Festival Hall in London with the London Symphony
Orchestra. Del Newman was to conduct. I took my
own rhythm section with me.

A few weeks before the performance I went to
Tommy Nutter, who outfitted many of the English
stars. He had a tailor shop, Nutters, on Saville Row.

Tommy made me a beautiful white tuxedo with satin braiding and a vest. A Tommy suit meant that I was really making it.

As the day of the concert came nearer, I began to get nervous and developed psychosomatic illnesses. My throat tightened and closed up, my bronchial tubes felt irritated. I was virtually a basket case. Because I had never taken singing lessons, I sang from the chest instead of the diaphragm, and the strain often resulted in chronic bronchitis or tracheitis. This was a battle that lasted for years. A doctor examined me and found nothing wrong—I had no fever, no coughing or sneezing. But the pains were very real. I could not sing well. Unfortunately my throat specialists were in the United States and unavailable to me in this crisis—Dr. Roger Rose in New York and Dr. Hans Von Leden in Los Angeles.

Two days before the concert I was convinced I could not go on. I drove Leba and everyone around me crazy, and refused to go outside for fear I would catch a cold.

The night before the concert I couldn't sleep. I tried a hot toddy—tea, lemon, honey and a shot of cognac—but nothing seemed to help. I kept dreading the ordeal of standing on the stage of Festival Hall and belting out songs for two solid hours. At last, out of sheer exhaustion, I fell asleep.

When I opened my eyes it was morning—the day of the big concert. When I tried my voice, it was there. The question had been decided—I would go on.

As the day progressed, flowers arrived from various fans and friends, and the phone rang all morning with requests for tickets. In a few hours I would be onstage.

I almost looked forward to getting out there, getting the waiting over. The expectation was always worse than the performance.

At sound check and rehearsal that afternoon I was in for a shock. I'd psyched myself into thinking Festival Hall was an intimate room with only twenty or thirty seats. But now, with the hall completely lit up, I could see all 2,500 of them. My fingers were freezing, my voice shaky. We went through several numbers, and my temples and ears were beating so much that I could hardly hear the notes. Afterwards Leba and I returned to the flat.

At 7 P.M. a limousine picked us up and we drove in silence to Festival Hall. Outside the hall vendors were selling Neil Sedaka programs and T-shirts. As the limo pulled up in front of the stage door, my anxiety slowly faded.

The dressing room was actually a suite which included a banquet room where I could receive guests. Waiters were already setting up glasses and hors d'oeuvres. Soon a page knocked on my door and called, "Mr. Sedaka, five minutes please." Leba and I walked hand in hand backstage. "Neil," Leba told me, "enjoy this. This is what you worked for all these years in England. Let them see how good you are." The overture began, and the emcee introduced me. "Ladies and gentlemen, please welcome the many talents of Neil Sedaka."

As I walked out, the lights were blinding. I felt a sudden rush of excitement, and before I knew it I was into my opening song, "Sing Me." The applause as I finished was like a shot of adrenalin, and I launched into "Gone with the Morning," "Cardboard California," "Superbird," "Solitaire" and "Love Will Keep Us Together" with more energy than I had ever felt in my life. The crowd seemed to be right with me, loose, responsive, applauding louder with each song. As I finished with "Standing on the Inside," "Our Last Song Together," and "That's When the Music Takes Me," they jumped up yelling. Sweat was rolling down my face, and I felt as if I had just won a race—exhausted, relieved that the ordeal was over, and overjoyed at my triumph. Leba took me in her arms in the wings. And then the audience started chanting for an encore. Afterwards the banquet room was jammed with revelers from the record company, friends like Freddy Gershon who'd flown over, and a delightful surprise, Rex Harrison, who said "Neil, you were wonderful. I only have one question—why did everyone switch from acoustical music to these loud, electronic guitars? I thought 'Solitaire' and 'Hungry Years' were delightful because they didn't rely on electric guitars. You are one of the few people with the versatility to write both ways." It was said as only Rex Harrison could—witty but astute.

Photographers came backstage to take pictures, but Rex did not have his hairpiece on, and Margaret Gardner of Rogers and Cowan, my PR firm, was reluctant to allow any picture-taking. Rex, however, was obliging. Afterwards we went out to dinner together. After two hours onstage, I was ravenous.

This was the beginning of an annual major concert for me in London—twice more at Festival Hall and then a first: I played The Palladium solo—just me and the piano—and we sold out solid for the week.

PART IV
SEDAKA'S BACK
1974–

CHAPTER 23
LIFE WITH ELTON JOHN

Though I was still in eclipse in America, my career in England was red hot. I was performing in concert halls everywhere—the Fiestas in Stockton and Sheffield, Jollees in Stoke. Leba and I decided to give a big party to thank our many friends for making us so welcome in Britain.

The apartment was ablaze with fresh flowers and we hired a caterer for the evening. That night some of the biggest names in rock got together under my roof, including Elton John, The Carpenters, Linsey De Paul, Ron Wood, Rod Stewart, Paul McCartney and 10 cc. If a bomb had fallen on my apartment the record industry would have been devastated. We went through five cases of champagne, and none of us was feeling any pain. At 2 A.M. it was still going strong.

When people had cleared out somewhat, I quietly took Elton John and his manager, John Reid, aside.

"Elton," I said, "Fred Gershon, my friend and attorney, told me about a new venture you're starting in America—Rocket Records. Would you be interested in signing me to your company?"

Elton's eyes lit up. "Neil, I didn't know you were available. I think it's a great idea. With the success you've been having in England, I think it would be a cinch to launch you in America.

"Like handling gold bricks," John Reid said. "Elton, all we'd need is an endorsement from you. With you behind Neil, it's guaranteed. Maybe you could even write the liner notes on the LP. I think Neil could hit the top."

I was ecstatic to have enlisted the support of the biggest rock superstar since The Beatles. Elton smelled money—he really thought I had something. We all shook hands on the deal.

I signed a contract with Rocket Records, and Elton invited Leba and me to the famous Caribou Ranch, a recording studio in Colorado. Elton wanted to discuss my first album and single on Rocket Records.

The studio sat high in the Colorado mountains, surrounded by magnificent rolling hills and trees. Each guest had an individual log cabin, very modern and well furnished. There was an old-style mess hall where visiting recording artists ate with their bands and guests. Leba and I sat with Elton and his producer Gus Dudgeon. In the afternoons Leba and I took long walks and went horseback riding through the wilderness. Elton was recording a new album, and he and Gus

Dudgeon spent a great deal of time in the studio. Gus was a real perfectionist, and the recording of "Lucy in the Sky" seemed to go on forever. In between takes Elton and the band and I played billiards and pinball. There was great excitement in the air.

When Elton's work was finished, he left with Leba and me. "I'm going to underdress for this plane trip," he said. But when we left for the airport to catch a plane, Elton's conception of a modest outfit proved to be a gold lamé suit, sparkling red shoes, a long bright-colored scarf, a fancy white walking stick, a white pan-ama hat, and red glasses to match his shoes. Everyone at the airport was agog.

John Reid, Elton's manager, had arranged for a pre-paid ticket. The girl behind the ticket counter, though, apparently didn't recognize Elton—despite his unusual costume—and asked for identification. The English are known not to carry any cards on them. There were a couple of awkward moments between Elton and this girl.

"I must have some sort of ID, sir, before I can issue you your ticket."

She must have come from Outer Mongolia or Mars.

"I have a diary," Elton said, pulling it out. "Here, take a look at it. I write in it every day."

"Sir, I'm sorry, this is not identification."

By this time it seemed everyone in the airport was staring at us. Elton finally paid with cash to save fur-ther embarrassment.

On the plane, Elton said, "You have carte blanche on the choice of songs for your Rocket album." I suggested a compilation of songs from both the English LP, *The*

Tra-la Days Are Over with 10 cc, and the Robert Appere L.A. sessions. I finally chose "Standing on the Inside," "Music," "Sad Eyes," "Love Will Keep Us Together," "Solitaire," "Laughter in the Rain," "The
Immigrant," "Our Last Song Together," "Little
Brother" and "The Way I Am."

"What do you think we ought to release as a single?"
he asked me.

"Laughter in the Rain," I replied without hesitation.
"It's doing well in England."

"I agree—'Laughter in the Rain' then. I think you're
right about the liner notes. Something by me might call
attention to it at the radio stations. I think I'll also visit
some of the stations. This is, after all, the first of my
Rocket Records."

Elton was often asked to be a guest disc jockey.
Radio fans loved it. They called him "EJ the DJ."

"I would also like to consider the possibility of using
you as the opening act in some of my arena concerts."

This was the chance of a lifetime for me.

"It's mutually beneficial," he said. "If your records
take off, they'll help launch Rocket as a label."

The photo session for the cover of the album took
place at the home Elton was renting in Beverly Hills.
"You look like a heavy Al Pacino," John Reid told me
at the session. I was 172 pounds in 1975.

"Listen, I have a great idea," John said. "Why don't
you wear a black pinstriped suit, a hat, and hold a long
cigar. Sort of a parody of the Godfather look."

The proof of the cover came back looking quite dramatic, after a few minor miracles with the air brush
(shading my double chin). John Reid liked the title

The Tra-la Days Are Over, but after seeing the cover, we decided to call it *Sedaka's Back*.

After several anxious days, the first test pressing arrived at home in Merriewold. As I put it on the record player, my heart was beating a mile a minute. I had waited for this moment for years. I placed the needle on side one and held my breath. The sound was wonderful—crisp and clear and contemporary. Each cut seemed stronger than the last. When I got to "Laughter in the Rain," I screamed with joy—everything was perfect—melody, lyric, mood, feeling, romance. I knew in my heart that it would be gold. I could hardly sleep the two weeks before it was released.

A few days later, as Leba and I were driving into Manhattan to visit our accountants, I heard, to my shock, "Laughter in the Rain" on the car radio. But it was *not* me singing. I pulled the car over and listened carefully. When the song was finished, the DJ announced, "That was a new artist, Lea Roberts, singing 'Laughter in the Rain.' "

My heart sank. My record was being released in ten days. Someone else had beaten me to the punch with my own song! And her version was really terrific. I felt my comeback flying out the window.

When someone wants to record a new song, no permission from the writer is necessary. They merely ask for a license from the publisher. The writer is paid a royalty on the sale of the record, sheet music and radio and TV play. If this woman's record of "Laughter" became a hit, my chance for a comeback would be destroyed—perhaps forever. I couldn't sit by and let this happen.

I called John Reid and told him the situation. He asked me to fly out to L.A. to talk with the heads of MCA Records. MCA distributed Elton's Rocket label. I booked my flight for the following day.

Johnny Muso of MCA, after listening to my record of "Laughter in the Rain," said he thought it had a great shot at being a hit.

"There is a new recording of 'Laughter in the Rain' on the United Artists label by a Lea Roberts," I explained. "We've got to push up our release date before she gets too much air play."

Johnny Muso agreed. Instead of ten days, he made the release date five days away.

My version of "Laughter in the Rain" came out early in 1975, at the same time as my LP, *Sedaka's Back.* Both were reviewed in all the music trade periodicals, including *Cash Box, Billboard* and *Record World.* Full page ads were taken out which included Elton's liner notes. In three days, my recording of "Laughter" was playing all over the country. The Lea Roberts record was dead.

I bought the latest trades and began to circle the new records being added to radio stations each week. There were no less than twelve listings for "Laughter." I also looked through the tip sheets, inside reports to the industry that predict what is happening in the current record market across the country. All three sheets, *Radio and Records* magazine, the *Gavin Sheet*, and *Kal Rudman's Report*, predicted that "Laughter" would be a hit. I wrote a postcard thanking the program director of each radio station that played it. Sales started at the rate of two and three thousand copies each day. Not good enough.

After watching the charts with mounting frustration, I came home and saw a note pasted on the front door. It was from my son, Marc: "CONGRATULATIONS, DAD. 'LAUGHTER' HAS ENTERED THE TOP 100 AT NUMBER 92."

After almost ten years of silence in America, I was back on the charts. I took the note off the front door and walked in the house with tears in my eyes. It was happening—though how big the comeback would be, I was not sure yet.

CHAPTER 24
NO. 1

I celebrated my thirty-sixth birthday as the single of "Laughter in the Rain" climbed the national charts, rising about eight places each week. This was the usual pattern with a ballad, and the right way to pick up steady sales. But it went too slowly for my taste. I kept thinking sales were going to taper off. The only play thus far in New York was on an easy listening station, WNEW-AM, that featured mostly Sinatra and Ella Fitzgerald. It had an older audience that usually didn't buy records; still, it was a start.

The LP *Sedaka's Back* was not selling. As this was my first LP in several years, the distributors were waiting to see what would happen to the single before they'd put the LP in a prominent place in the retail stores.

Then, to my alarm, Elton decided I would not be his opening act. Elton's associate, Connie Pappas, explained to me, "Elton's audience is too frenzied and too devoted. They wouldn't pay attention to your act—or any opening act before Elton." I was disappointed but had to agree. Kiki Dee, the next artist to be signed to Rocket Records, was made the opening act instead.

I had an engagement in England for three weeks, doing clubs, concerts and a TV show, and several American entrepreneurs and managers flew over to meet with Leba and me during the tour. It was time for me to sign with a manager now that things were happening in the States. Of all of them, I liked best a young guy named Elliot Abbott, who was with BNB, a management firm with many important clients, including Karen and Richard Carpenter. Elliott seemed to understand the artistic temperament very well. He had been Jim Croce's manager and close friend and had been called to identify Jim's body when the terrible plane accident occurred. I liked Elliott's unassuming manner.

That night, after meeting with Elliot Abbott, Leba and I had dinner in London with Joan Collins and her husband, Ron Cass. They lived in a house a block away from our flat, and Joan's two children by Anthony Newley were the same age as Dara and Marc and had become good friends with them. On Sundays Joan would take all the children down to Chelsea for ceramic classes.

When we met at Ron and Joan's for cocktails, Rod Stewart and Britt Ekland were there. Joan had invited them to join us for dinner, along with their friends, Evie and Leslie Bricusse. We went to Tiberio's for din-

ner and Britt, who had only been seeing Rod for a short
time, was falling all over him, to the embarrassment of
everyone at the table. When she was not fawning over
Rod, she was reprimanding Evie Bricusse for putting
on weight. I thought Evie to be an incredibly attractive
woman. Britt insisted on ordering chicken for Evie,
while we had pastas and wonderful Italian delicacies.
Poor Evie picked on a piece of roast chicken all night.
As she ate, Britt continued harping at her. "I am your
friend and I must tell you," she said, "you put on so
much weight."

Finally, I could not take it any more. "Leave her
alone, Britt. I think she's gorgeous and has a wonderful
body. She looks like a woman should."

At last Britt shut up and contented herself with
mauling Rod Stewart, practically undressing him at the
table. A quiet dinner it was not.

The following week while attending a Royal Command Performance of the film *Funny Lady*, I met Barbra Streisand for the first time since *The Ed Sullivan
Show*. Streisand was now at the peak of her career and
I'd always admired her magnificent voice and her tremendous talent.

I had never attended a Royal Command Performance
before. The chauffeured Rolls-Royces pulled up in
front of the theater, disgorging people dressed in tux-
edos and gowns. Before the movie began, all the VIPs
were ushered into a small anteroom adjacent to the
main theater. There we were to wait for Streisand, Jon
Peters and finally Queen Elizabeth.

Photographers were everywhere and the sweat
poured down my back. Even after so many years of

meeting other celebrities, this time I was really nervous. I finally got up the nerve to introduce myself to Streisand. I asked if I might have a picture with her. She said, "No!" and turned abruptly—and just as abruptly turned back and said, "You're Neil Sedaka! I love 'Laughter in the Rain.' " My heart beat again. She then summoned the photographers herself, and we took a picture together. We exchanged a few words and I was still numb from the excitement when a few minutes later Queen Elizabeth walked in. Streisand, unaware of protocol, committed a royal gaffe. No one is supposed to talk to the Queen unless she addresses you first. But Streisand, upon being introduced, impulsively asked the Queen, "Why do you always wear gloves?" Her Majesty explained that the custom went back to medieval times when knights wore sharp armor.

When Leba and I returned to New York, "Laughter" was still creeping up the charts—it was now in the 20s, and still going strong. The sales were slow but increasing steadily, selling about four or five thousand a day. Most of the big Top 40 stations in the major cities were playing it, though there was still no significant New York play. New York is always the last to get behind a record.

Every Wednesday was a chart day, the day we found out what the next week's position would be. I lived from Wednesday to Wednesday. *Billboard* was my New York Stock Exchange.

Elton called me from the road occasionally to calm me down and reassure me. One night, however, Elton called at 3 A.M. needing my help to calm *him* down.

"Neil, am I waking you?"

"Who is this?" I said, half asleep.

"It's Elton. I'm calling from Los Angeles. I need your advice. I have a concert tomorrow night with over 30,000 people and my voice is awful. I don't know what to do. My throat feels like sandpaper."

"The first thing to do is to remain calm. Take hot steam inhalations—stay in the shower until the room is filled with steam. Try hot tea with lemon, honey and brandy. That's good for the throat. Gargle with hot salt water and, at all costs, don't go any place where you have to shout to be heard. You'll be all right." He took my advice and came through with flying colors.

Elton was genuinely happy about my "Laughter," and on his guest disc jockey appearances he always plugged my record. The radio people were very impressed. Elton was King and whatever he said was law. "Laughter" finally appeared on Top 10 charts in smaller cities. I called Rocket Records daily. The sales were up to eight and ten thousand a day. When New York's big teenage station, WABC, finally played it, I had reached a turning point. *Radio and Records* magazine listed it as a "Breaker" on their back page—I made Bill Gavin's Top 30 and Kal Rudman's list on his all-important first red page.

While in L.A. to do press and television, as usual I stayed at the Beverly Hills Hotel, but this time the hotel staff recognized my name—a welcome change from four years before.

Poolside on a Sunday at the Beverly Hills is a show. The beautiful women and men of Hollywood strut around flaunting their wares. Celebrities of all kinds are paged on the loudspeakers. Some go so far as to page themselves so everyone is aware of their presence.

During an interview with Cleveland Amory, the columnist, I noticed familiar faces in the cabana next to mine. It was Don and Sheila Kirshner. After the interview Don asked me to join them. Donnie now had his own television show, *Don Kirshner's Rock Concert*, which was only a few months old. Showing him the "Laughter" position on the charts, I said, "Donnie, since you are the publisher of "Laughter," why don't you put me on your show? It's going to be a hit."

I'll never forget his reply: "Neil, I have bigger plans for you. The timing isn't right, now. However, if you can get Elton to do a few songs, I'll put you both on the show."

I was livid. "In other words, you won't put me on without Elton?"

"That's right," he replied.

Walking away from him I dove into the pool. Don turned to Leba. "Neil just swam away from me."

Leba said, "Forever, Donnie."

Peter Sellers was at the pool the following day. He said to me, "Your records seem to bring me out of deep depressions. They're inspiring." He invited us to a screening of his new movie that night. He was with a stunning girl named Titi, the Swedish ambassador's daughter. When we arrived, it was evident he had been taking advantage of the liquid refreshment available. The film was long and boring, and when it came to a close, Peter was drunk. We made our way next door to an Italian restaurant, where a pianist began playing dinner music. Sellers insisted that I get up and play.

"No, really Peter, I can't. It just wouldn't be appropriate."

He was adamant, turning to me angrily and saying, "You schmuck. I made a fool of myself in the film. Now let's see you make an ass of yourself at the piano." I refused.

We ate a quick, uncomfortable dinner and left.

"Laughter in the Rain" rose to the teens on the charts. I wanted a Top 10 desperately. When it hit number 10, I wanted a Top 5 record. Finally it hit number 3, where it stayed for a while. Was there more strength in it?

I was now enough of a celebrity in the U.S. that the talk shows started to request me. I had never done any before. Over the next few weeks I did them all: Carson, Douglas, Griffin, Dinah, and *Midnight Special.* I would work myself up to a nervous pitch, and by the time I was in front of the cameras, sitting on the panel, my mouth was dry, my lips parched, and my mind racing. Although to the viewer I seemed to be in control, in fact I felt as though someone had beaten me up. Merv was gracious and smooth, and his musical knowledge made me feel more at home. Carson was sharp and witty. Dinah Shore and I sang "Solitaire" together.

The night of *Midnight Special,* Connie Pappas and John Reid came to the show. Before showtime, John caught my arm. "Sit down, Neil." He had a sly look in his eye. Handing me a jewelry box, he said "Go ahead. Open it." Inside was a charm in the shape of a disc which read: "Congratulations. You are #1 in *Cash*

Box, Billboard and *Record World.* [Signed] Rocket Records."

"Ya-hoo," I screamed. I jumped and I cried. After ten years, I was back at number 1 with a totally new style.

The next day Dick Fox, my agent, asked me to accept an offer to perform three evenings at the Troubador in L.A., one of the top rock clubs in the world. I collected a group of great musicians—David Foster on keyboards, Leeland Sklar on bass, Russ Kunkel on drums, Dean Parks and Danny Kooch on guitars, and Brian and Brenda Russell and Abigail Haness on vocals—and Robert Appere helped with the sound.

Half of Hollywood would be in the audience that night. As Leba and I were dressing at the bungalow, the disc jockey on KHJ said, "Folks, here's the new number 1 song in the country—"Laughter in the Rain." Leba and I cried and danced around like two idiots. At last we got in the car and drove off to meet Neil Diamond, who was taking us to dinner with his wife Marsha.

The audience at the Troubador included James Taylor, Carly Simon, Andy Williams, the Neil Diamonds and Elton John. Most of the program was from the *Sedaka's Back* album. At the end there was an emotional scene—a standing ovation—and then everyone rushed back to the dressing room to celebrate.

My comeback was now news. There were more interviews than I could handle, even seeing several reporters a day. All of my songs now seemed to be on the air at once. If it wasn't me singing, it was another artist's recording of one of my songs. Then the personal

appearance offers started coming in. I got a band together, and the heavy touring began.

Touring in a private jet, I did forty weeks of
one-nighters in 1975. The brutal pace drove me to
drink—two vodka martinis and a half bottle of wine
every night. The other members of the band smoked
marijuana, so I started again, too, though never before a
show.

I ate my dinner at midnight after the last concert, always fried and greasy food. And again before I went to
sleep, lots of wine to ease the tension. I'd wake up in
the morning still groggy from the night before. We'd
shoot out to the jet about three in the afternoon, smoke
a joint, and have a bloody mary or two on the plane.
When I arrived in the next city, I'd crash out for an
hour, get up at 7 P.M., shower, shave, wash my hair, and
go back out to face the next audience. This went on
night after night, week after week. Why would any
sane human being do this to himself? The same reason
we all work: when we know the money is there we
want to take it. Who can say that it will always be
there?

Thank God for Leba and the kids. When I went
home for a break, they were a great stabilizing effect.
Without the tension and pressure of concerts, TV, and
interviews, I didn't drink as much at home.

CHAPTER 25

DARA AND MARC

I was happy to see that our daughter Dara was already completely taken with music. Perhaps it was the result of my singing to Leba's belly when she was pregnant with Dara. More likely it was the piano lessons and growing up with a singer for a dad. Dara could sing a major third above any note on the scale I picked. We used to listen to records together at home. Her favorites were Stevie Wonder and Chaka Khan and rhythm and blues.

My son Marc had become a whiz at video and electronics. He called me out into the backyard at Merriewold one day and set off a rocket he'd made out of wood. It soared a respectable distance and then sprouted a parachute he'd devised for a graceful ride back to earth.

When we were in New York, Dara and Marc loved
to spend time with their grandfather, Mac Sedaka, or
Poppa, as they called him.

My sister Ronnie's family had moved to Las Vegas.
Mac had practically raised her kids. Gary and Barry
adored Mac and no wonder—he gave his time to them
unselfishly, teaching them tennis, golf, bowling and
fishing.

He had been driving a cab for thirty years, sometimes working through the night so his wife and children would have everything they wanted.

On two occasions I was horrified to hear that he had
been mugged by passengers and said, "Dad, would you
like to retire to Florida?"

He was overjoyed, knowing at last he was going to be
able to enjoy life to the fullest.

One day he came home to discover a note from
Eleanor explaining that she was off to Florida for the
weekend "to look for a house." She chose it without
Mac, as usual.

Mac loved the house, and they settled in Fort Lauderdale. Marc went down for a visit, and when he returned with home movies of the trip, he ran them for
us. "The amazing thing about Poppa is laughter," Marc
said. "When Poppa is around he can lighten any situation. Here's a scene coming on now that Gary shot
when Barry was leaving Florida. Watch what happens.
Nana is crying in the background but there's Poppa
saying, 'Barry is leaving. We are bringing him to the
airport. He-he-he.' "

Leba spoke pensively. "There's nothing complicated

about Poppa. His sensitivity and honest directness seem to put everyone at ease. Maybe that's why everyone wants to be with him."

After a week's rest with Leba and Dara and Marc at Merriewold I'd run for the jet and be off on the road again. My weight had soared to 180. I was often dizzy and short of breath. But being on the stage was now more natural to me than being off it. I came to crave applause and instant approval like a drug. Accompanying this over-amped state was a strange obsession to suffer, to set up obstacles, to make things harder for myself. I actually looked for new things to worry about.

Still quaking over the trauma of my professional life falling apart after The Beatles, I lived in constant fear that my career would bottom out again. I was becoming psychologically punchy. The love I got from audiences at concerts somehow created a need to be loved more intensely offstage and with that came the self-doubts. I began to question if I really liked myself. "How good *am* I?" I would ask myself. I was embarrassed to meet people offstage, fearing they'd say, "He's not so good. He's clever. It's just a well-put-together trick." When I went I into a restaurant, I would look to see if I was recognized. When I wasn't, I took it as a sign of box-office doom.

My last engagement in 1975 was a TV show with Dick Clark. By the time I arrived in L.A. for the taping, I had been on the road for six months. I was the host for the show, and it was strenuous work that left me ill and exhausted.

The next morning I visited Dr. Charles Koviwitz. My blood pressure was high and my general health poor. He insisted on no more than two drinks a night— and a long rest.

Leba and I had wanted a large apartment in Manhattan for a long time. Leba found a beauty on the corner of Seventy-second Street and Fifth Avenue, a tastefully decorated seven-room apartment that was worth waiting for. It was a real showplace. The first day we moved in, I wrote on the note board in the kitchen, "This is to die from." The apartment included a marble entrance foyer, a library, a living room that was all pastel silks, needlepoint and Aubussons, three spacious bedrooms with their own baths, and a formal dining room—a far cry from Brighton Beach.

The first person I invited over to show it off to was Barry Manilow, who lived down the street. We had been good friends since I had first tried to hire him at the suggestion of my agent years ago. I had called Barry looking for someone to help me with a couple of arrangements, and he was a young, bright new arranger who had worked for Bette Midler as a pianist and conductor. He was just beginning his own career, and didn't have time then. We did keep in touch with each other, though.

Barry was always concerned about being seen in public, feeling that big stars must remain aloof, and surrounded himself with security people and guard dogs. At first I was surprised because it seemed so unlike Barry. But he was convinced he might be attacked by admiring fans on the street. Barry is a good singer, but a Burt Reynolds he's not. I think he actually wanted to draw attention. Stardom has a way of playing havoc with a person's head.

CHAPTER 26
THE
CARPENTERS

After weeks of rest my health was back to normal. Karen and Richard Carpenter, clients of BNB, were about to embark on a six-week tour, beginning on the East Coast in open-air theaters, continuing to Vegas, and finally to Japan. Elliott told me that Richard wanted me as their opening act. Elliott recommended it—The Carpenters played to my kind of audience. "Also," he said, "*Sedaka's Back* is still not selling despite 'Laughter's' number one position and a tour might help." I agreed.

Richard created a very clever show, combining a number of familiar old hits with more current material. I was to come on at the beginning of the show and do thirty-five minutes, and return to the stage at the end to sing several encores with Karen and Richard.

We opened the tour at Ben Segal's Oakdale Music Theatre in the Round in Wallingford, Connecticut. At our first show I was a nonstop bundle of energy from start to finish and the audience was cheering all the way. Then Karen and Richard came on to do their portion of the program. Karen had an exquisite voice, and their songs and music were tasteful and musically superb. Richard's piano was the perfect complement to this beautiful, mellow, romantic music. However in contrast to my thirty-five minutes, their act was quiet and subdued. Everything sounded the same, whereas my songs were varied. You could sense the difference in the audience's response. They were appreciative, but unexcited, and The Carpenters received only mild applause. While I was obviously thrilled to be onstage, The Carpenters seemed to walk through the act.

When the first reviews came out in the Connecticut papers, they were polite to The Carpenters and raved about me. They called it the surprise of the year. Ben Segal had to hide the reviews from Karen and Richard.

We went on to the Garden State Art Center in New Jersey, Pine Nob in Detroit, and the Ravinia Festival in Chicago. *The New York Daily News* headlined: SEDAKA STEALS SHOW FROM CARPENTERS. As beautifully as Karen and Richard performed, I thought their music was a carbon copy of their recorded versions. Although each note was polished, to me it sounded sterile and unemotional. I was a big fan of theirs, but I had to admit that the audience was not moved. The most popular section of their set was the finale, when Karen and Richard and I appeared onstage for the duets and trios.

Unsurprisingly, I began to detect some resentment.

When we arrived at The Riviera Hotel in Las Vegas for a two-week engagement, we played to a packed house, including such celebrities as Glen Campbell and Paul Anka. The audience cheered each of my songs, and by the end I had them on their feet. By the second night Richard decided to take out the finale—he said the show was running too long. The third night, Dick Clark called me to say he was coming to the show, as did Tom Jones, and during the show I introduced them to the audience. When I left the stage I heard Richard Carpenter screaming, "Get that son of a bitch out!" Karen, about to go on, was in tears. "Neil, I'm so sorry about this," she said. She looked painfully thin, and weighed only about ninety pounds.

The next morning Elliott called. "Neil, Richard wants to call it quits. He would like you to leave the tour today."

I was shocked. "I can't believe it," I told him.

I called the group in and told them the news—we were to pack up that afternoon. My name was to be removed from the marquee of the Riviera Hotel.

When Wayne Newton heard, he called to ask if he could do anything for me. "It's so unfair," he said. Eydie Gormé and Steve Lawrence promised to make an announcement during their show. "You're being fired because you're too good," Steve told me.

I called my friend Alan Carr, a famed producer and show business manager, and told him what had happened.

"Neil, you must call a press conference in Vegas. You must let the public know what really happened. Make this work for you. Above all, before you leave, let

Elliott rebook you in Vegas as a headliner at the Riviera Hotel."

I followed his advice. The next day, after the press conference, stories appeared in the U.P.I. and A.P. wires stating "SEDAKA FIRED FOR BEING TOO STRONG." DJs picked up on the incident as well, and The Carpenters looked bad. While my records continued to do well on the air, The Carpenters' records were often followed by snide remarks from DJs. Before I left Las Vegas, Elliott had arranged for the new contract—I was to return to the Riviera in a few months as a headliner and I have been working there eight weeks a year ever since.

A few days later Karen Carpenter was hospitalized. In her worn-down condition, this had been too much for her. She was in a state of depression. The Carpenters cancelled their Japanese tour.

I think if Richard had realized the repercussions, he might have kept me on the tour. Since then, on the few occasions I have met The Carpenters, we have always been cordial to each other.

After this incident I had no recourse but to leave BNB. Since Elliott Abbott was the reason I'd gone there in the first place, I suggested we form our own management company. Leba and he became partners in Renaissance Management. Among the clients, besides myself, were Randy Newman, Ry Cooder and Kim Carnes.

CHAPTER 27
THE CAPTAIN
AND TENNILLE

Sedaka's Back finally made the LP charts thanks to a smart promotion man named Dennis Morgan. Now it was time to think of a follow-up to "Laughter in the Rain."

After many months I narrowed down the choice to "The Immigrant" or "Love Will Keep Us Together," two very different kinds of songs. Howie Greenfield had written the lyric to "Love Will Keep Us Together," and Phil Cody the lyric for "The Immigrant." With my new image, I was leaning toward "The Immigrant." It was an interesting, poetic work, quite different for a pop song.

> Harbors open their arms
> To the young, searching foreigner
> Come to live in the light
> Of the beacon of Liberty.

"Love Will Keep Us Together," on the other hand, was a light piece of fluff, like marshmallow creme, with a corny lyric, but one that would appeal to the mass market. The tune was a combination of old Supremes, old Beach Boys and Al Green.

I played both for dozens of friends and colleagues, trying to make up my mind. The choice was crucial, as it would dictate the future sales of my records to a great extent. After deliberation I decided on "The Immigrant."

Before cutting "The Immigrant" in 1975 I decided to dedicate it to John Lennon because of the trouble he was having with the American Government. John Lennon and I had met at several parties in New York and Los Angeles through Elton John, a close friend of his. I was in awe of this musical giant. Though Paul McCartney had always been my favorite of The Beatles, it was John Lennon's genius that contributed so greatly to their success. In 1975 the United States refused to give him the "green card" that would enable him to stay in the country, because of his past history with drugs and radical politics. I felt that John Lennon was a great human being who should be welcomed into the United States with open arms.

When I told John I wanted to dedicate my song to him, which I was introducing on Dick Clark's *American Bandstand*, John said he was immensely flattered. After the TV show was over I received a call from John: "I thought the song was beautiful. Yoko and I were watching and we loved it."

Later John agreed to a request from WNEW-FM radio in New York to do a live three-way phone interview with me in conjunction with the record. John was one of the most gracious rock celebrities I've ever encountered.

Both "The Immigrant" and The Captain and Tennille recording of "Love Will Keep Us Together" came out about the same time. The Captain and Tennille, a new duo, heard my song on the LP and decided to record it as their debut single. I kept saying to myself, "Please let 'The Immigrant' be bigger." Although I had written both songs, "The Immigrant" was the more important to me at that moment in my career. I had had a lot of hit songs to my credit done by other singers and having yet another would not be nearly as crucial to my performing career as the success of a song I had recorded myself. I was grateful, however, that The Captain and Tennille, at the end of their version, sang the line "Sedaka's back." I thought that was a wonderful thing to do.

Unfortunately, the United States at the time "The Immigrant" was released was flooded with Southeast Asians fleeing the war in Vietnam and Cambodia, and the public was not particularly overjoyed with a song dealing with the subject. "The Immigrant" went as high as number 22, and soon "Love Will Keep Us Together" passed it by. "Love" eventually went directly to number 1, and stayed there for several weeks, taking the Grammy as Most Performed Song of 1976—with all kinds of other Grammy nominations. Their record *was* great, but, did I make the wrong decision!

Fortunately, *Sedaka's Back* began picking up sales and after staying on the LP charts for 54 weeks, sold 850,000 copies.

I still kicked myself, though, for giving up "Love Will Keep Us Together." It was my own fault. The only person who had urged me to put it out over "The Immigrant" was my mother-in-law, Esther, who is tone-deaf. "Neil," she said, "I like that song. It is 1976 and it *is* love that keeps people together, nothing else. No contracts, no marriage licenses." She was right.

CHAPTER 28
BETTE MIDLER

Bette Midler is the most exciting performer in show business, hands down. It was tremendously exciting to do a big TV special with her as my guest in 1976. Bette and I sang a duet, "Lunch Will Keep Us Together," a spoof of my Grammy winner. Bette as usual raised the roof.

Carol Bayer Sager was a friend of Bette's and one evening after the special, Leba and I had a surprise visit from Carol, Bette and Richard Perry, the record producer.

Bette is just the opposite of what she portrays in front of the public. She is a shy, quiet, sweet girl. Everytime we meet her we marvel at the transformation that occurs when she's performing. She relaxed in our apartment that night, sitting on the floor with no makeup, hair in ponytail. I sat at the Baldwin playing old rock 'n' roll songs while Bette and Richard Perry sang along. I kept thinking, "Is this the same Bette Midler who stands on stage cursing and throwing herself through wild gyrations?"

Bette was giving a rare appearance the following week at the Copacabana in New York City. Leba and I were invited by Jerry Edelstein, who is the attorney for both Bette and myself. Bette Midler is an incredible performer who has no inhibitions onstage. She screams out the notes with an abandon unequalled in entertainment history.

Aaron Russo, her manager at the time, said "Bette would love to see you after the performance." We were surprised. We thought after such an exhausting performance Bette would choose not to see anyone for at least an hour. Aaron walked us into the dressing room. There, in a robe, hair back in a ponytail, was the Bette who was there at our house the week before. We congratulated her on her performance. We said we would come back and bring our daughter, Dara, to see her.

Bette said, "Oh, no. I'll be so nervous. Don't tell me when you're bringing Dara. She sings wonderfully. I'll be so nervous." The mystery of artists—how do you explain it? Midler is a tiny dynamo on stage but in private—sedate, shy, polite—vulnerable.

I was horrified to see how much weight I was putting on with the return of the good life. When I toured Canada I was looking like a fat pig. The press called me "The Disco Doughboy," "A bowling pin with a smile button for a face," and "The most unlikely looking rock 'n' roll star." On the other hand, when *Time* magazine did an article on the "come-back kids," including Paul Anka and Frankie Valli, the author wrote, "Sedaka is everything that punky rock 'n' roll is not. He is civilized, intelligent and articulate."

A month later I released a third single from *Sedaka's Back* called "That's When the Music Takes Me." It was the first song for which I had written not only the music, but the lyrics. After all the years of collaboration with fine lyricists, I had been afraid to tackle lyrics. Carol Bayer Sager, however, had kept urging me to try, insisting I would have no trouble. So one night in Merriewold, when Leba and I were supposed to attend a party at a friend's house, I decided to give it a try. I told Leba to go to the party by herself. Alone, I sat at the menacing looking piano. There was a stash of powerful marijuana in the house. I rolled a joint and took a couple of drags and two hours later "That's When the Music Takes Me" was nearly finished. I was so afraid the marijuana had distorted my judgment that I had to wait until the following morning to decide whether it was really good.

When *Billboard* magazine published their annual poll in 1976, I had come in second to Elton John in the male vocalist category. "Music Takes Me" was in the 20s on the charts but was still struggling. I wrote postcards to radio stations, hoping this might influence air time, and appeared on endless interviews, but nothing seemed to work.

The most powerful man in radio in 1976 was Paul Drew, who was in charge of programming at the RKO radio chain—the largest chain of stations geared towards the teenage audience. A record played by Paul was an automatic candidate for a Top 10 position. John Reid and Elton were close friends with Paul Drew, and each week I called Rocket Records to see if the RKO chain had added "Music Takes Me." Each week the answer was no. Finally, a call came from John Reid.

"Sit down, Neil, I have some news for you. Paul has added your record—but not 'When the Music Takes Me'. He's added a cut off one of your English albums—'Bad Blood.' "

I was shocked. Here I had a record in the twenties on the charts, and RKO was adding an unreleased record to their play lists.

"Bad Blood" had had odd beginnings. In 1976 I had written a new collection of songs for my second LP on Rocket which included lyrics by Howie Greenfield, Phil Cody and myself. When it came time to record "Bad Blood," I thought it might be even more effective as a duet. I told Robert Appere at Clover Studios, "I want to ask Elton if he'll sing it with me in the studio."

"Yes! If Elton will agree to accompany you, this could be your biggest single yet." To my delight Elton was receptive to the idea.

We recorded the song in L.A. with the musicians, and space was left open for Elton. On the day Elton was set to record, the session was booked and Robert and I waited on pins and needles for him to arrive. I was afraid he had changed his mind, and the recording would fall through. At last Elton arrived, an hour and a half late, in a large, stretch Caddy limousine.

A hush fell over the studio as he walked in. After greeting everyone, Elton listened attentively to the background track as I sang. Then Elton went to the microphone. Elton has incredible ears, and he sang the background voice for "Bad Blood" in seven takes. When he left, Robert and I hugged each other. "Bad Blood," we knew, would be at the top of the charts.

When Paul Drew picked "Bad Blood" as the song RKO radio stations would play, records were not even available in the stores. Rocket rushed the single out in a matter of days, and stations all across the country jumped on it. It debuted in the Top 100 at number 62, a phenomenal entry, and went in the following weeks to numbers 26, 10, 5, 3 and finally, number 1, selling 1.4 million copies. It was, as Robert and I had predicted, my biggest success ever.

My second LP with Rocket Records was entitled *The Hungry Years*, which had been released in England under the title *Overnight Success*. The album included such songs as "Crossroads," "Lonely Night," "Stephen," "Bad Blood," "Your Favorite Entertainer," "N.Y. City Blues," "The Hungry Years" and a remake of "Breaking Up Is Hard To Do." I had discovered over the years that "Breaking Up" worked very well as a slow ballad, and it was as a slow ballad that I rereleased it. As *The Hungry Years* achieved gold status, with over 500,000 copies sold, I decided to follow up the single of "Bad Blood" with "Breaking Up." It, too, became a Top 10 hit. I was told it was the first time in pop music a singer had rerecorded the same song in a new style and each time had a hit.

Now that I was headlining in Las Vegas, I hired Artie Butler to rewrite my charts and to accompany me to the Vegas engagement as conductor. Before this, I had a crude piece of paper which I referred to when I rehearsed the orchestras alone.

CHAPTER 29
LIZA MINNELLI

When I play in Las Vegas I have a certain phobia about celebrities in the audience. I prefer that no one tell me who is there before the show, as it makes me nervous. When I walk off for my bows just before my closing, my road manager always tells me what celebrities are in the house so I can introduce them.

One night as I was playing at the Hilton Hotel, John Cowley told me, as I walked off before the bow, that Liza Minnelli was in the audience. It's always a compliment to an artist when a great star like Liza comes to see your show. She's an absolute dynamo on stage, with boundless energy and a great voice. I had met her years before when she was married to Peter Allen. I announced her that evening at the Hilton and the audience burst into wild applause. After the show she came backstage with her husband Mark. Liza is a warm and bubbly person and everyone finds themselves glued to her every move and word. "Watching you made me feel so . . . so good," Liza said. "I'd like to return the favor. Maybe I can do a third show Saturday night at the Riviera so you can see it."

Her road manager, turning to her, said, "Liza, you'll be exhausted. You've been on the road for the last two months. Are you sure you're up to a third show?"

"I want to do it for Neil and for the kids on the Strip."

It was a beautiful gesture and I was dying to see her new act. When the word got out that Liza was doing an extra show the excitement spread across the Vegas Strip. After finishing my second show at the Hilton that Saturday, I rushed over to the Riviera Hotel, and it was jam-packed with people. My friends and I were seated at Liza's table in the Versailles showroom. A few minutes before Liza was to walk out, however, her road manager came over to our table.

"Liza wants to see you before the show. She's a nervous wreck."

Liza's dressing room was like a steamroom. You could almost grow plants in it. She had several humidifiers going and the air conditioners were completely turned off. Liza sat in front of her mirror with a worried look on her face. Catching sight of me, she jumped up impulsively and kissed me. "Neil, my voice is a disaster. I went to the doctor this morning with a bad throat. I don't know whether I'll be able to get through this last show."

She went into some strenuous vocal exercises, making peculiar sounds and motions. I was used to seeing this, but her road manager thought Liza was having a nervous breakdown. She paced back and forth in the dressing room, repeating over and over "I can't sing, I can't sing." She had us both convinced she could not make it past the first number. "Neil, who's out there?"

"Entertainers from the Strip," I said. "Friends." I felt badly for this frail, nervous-looking girl. Liza was a bundle of nerves. I tried to make light of the whole thing. But I could certainly empathize with her, having felt that panic many times before. When we got back to our seats, I told the others, "Don't worry about her. Watch what happens when she walks out onstage."

The house lights went down. The audience started to applaud as Liza walked out onstage. She began singing alone for the first bars, and then, one by one, her own fourteen musicians walked out onstage. There was a clamorous ovation. She sang an hour and a half, from 2:30 A.M. to 4 A.M. Her voice sounded a bit tired but she was still incredible. Liza Minnelli is in a class by herself.

CHAPTER 30
LAKE TAHOE

In 1976 I received five BMI awards, as well as Song of the Year. BMI, Broadcast Music Incorporated, logs radio and television performances of songs. Each time a song is aired by a radio or television station, they make a notation of the play. This award is given to the one hundred most frequently played each year. The five songs of mine that won in 1976 were "Laughter in the Rain," "Bad Blood," "Solitaire," "Love Will Keep Us Together," and "Lonely Night"—a personal best.

During one of my state fair appearances in Seattle, Holmes Hendrickson, who booked the shows for Harrah's Hotels, came backstage and asked me if I would like to open for The Smothers Brothers in Tahoe. I would do thirty-five minutes. Harrah's is a wonderful hotel and I readily agreed.

The performances went very well, though I bridled a bit at not being the headliner. Then one evening Tommy was stuck on Lake Tahoe in a boat whose motor had conked out. As I finished my usual act I could see a stage person waving frantically at me from the wings to stretch my act. After another half an hour, The Smothers Brothers finally came on—and just in time, for I was beginning to run out of material. But the audience loved me, and as a result Harrah's realized that I could be a headliner. In fact the next year and every year after, I was invited back to Harrah's.

Working at Harrah's is always a real joy, because they ensure that every detail is seen to. A Rolls-Royce, a cook and a maid, transportation in Bill Harrah's private jet, a villa on the lake, even free ski lift tickets. They even go so far as to remember what kind of whiskey each artist drinks.

Headlining at the Hilton in Vegas can be as heady as playing Harrah's. Leba and I went to see Elvis Presley at the Hilton, and though he was bloated and obviously in trouble with his life, he put on a big show. At one point Elvis stopped in the middle of a song and said, "Excuse me, I have to go the the bathroom." The show went right on; he was smart enough to know that he now required a whole stageful of musicians to back him up. Elvis was a caricature of his former self and it was sad to see a legendary star falling apart before our eyes.

After the show Leba and I went backstage to visit Elvis in his lavish suite of dressing rooms. He was there with his entourage, including his father and Linda Thompson. Elvis grabbed me and said, "Neil, I've been listening to all of your stuff. We're on the same wave length and the same label, RCA Victor." He then took me over to the piano and said, "I love gospel songs and I'm going to sing some for you." I joined in and we sang white gospel together for the good part of an hour.

Later, when I was headlining at the Hilton myself and occupying the same suite, Leba and I were relaxing after the performance one night when she produced a beautiful blue scarf from her purse. Elvis had given it to her the night we'd visited him in this room. Leba said, "I remember Elvis studying my dress and saying, 'I bet I have a scarf that would match your gown perfectly.' And he did. He went into the bedroom for a minute and when he rejoined us he was carrying this scarf. He put it around my neck and kissed me. A perfect gentleman."

My son Marc loved it when I played Harrah's because it meant we could spend time together swimming and camping and fishing. During one camping excursion he hurt his finger and I later received this letter from him which I framed and put up in my study. Mark was twelve years old at the time.

Dear Dad,

The times that I spend alone with you will go down as the best in my life. I can not express the emotions I feel towards you, nor the enjoyment that you give me. I realize that you are under pressure and I appreciate that you can take time to spend it with me. You are the kind of man that I admire and love, and I pray that I can be like you when I grow up. You are a wonderful inspiration for me and I love you for it.

Love,
Marc

P.S. I took your advice and soaked my finger on the plane. As you can see by the writing, it helped.

Dara was now a teenager, and quite naturally she was in love with Shaun Cassidy of *The Hardy Boys* TV series. While playing at the Universal Amphitheatre, I arranged a meeting for Dara with Shaun. Dara's heart was pounding a mile a minute as she introduced herself to him. Parker Stevenson, the co-star of *The Hardy Boys*, was there as well. By the end of the day, Dara was more taken with Parker. So much for the best-laid plans. Fortunately Parker and I struck an immediate rapport, and became very good friends.

CHAPTER 31
TROUBLE WITH ELTON JOHN

Elton John was beginning to lose interest in me. My third LP for his Rocket Records was called *Steppin' Out*. My deal with Rocket was for three LPs and it looked like this would be my Rocket swan song.

Our relations were strained lately. I didn't know why. Elton surrounded himself with hangers-on of every description. They were party people out for good times. Elton was generous and gave elaborate gifts. It meant nothing for him to walk into Van Cleef & Arpels, which he called "the candy store," or Cartier's or Tiffany's or Hermes to buy thousands of dollars worth of trinkets and gifts for people. The stores often opened after hours so EJ could shop in privacy. He once gave me, as a token of our friendship, an $8,000 diamond-faced Tiffany watch. And when Leba mentioned she was collecting silver picture frames, Elton gave her a pair of beautiful Art Deco frames encrusted with semi-precious stones.

I sensed that Elton was ambivalent about supporting an entourage. He is clever enough to understand peoples' motives and to recognize the difference between friendship and ass kissing. To the hangers-on I represented a threat since I sincerely liked Elton and admired his genius and valued what I thought was a growing friendship. I'm sorry to say that these people may have repeated stories out of context and told out-and-out lies in order to break up our relationship. For whatever reason the friendship did end.

I appreciated what he had done for my career. I honestly believe that if it were not for the falsehoods that were manufactured by these insecure cronies, I would still be close to Elton today.

Steppin' Out was my final LP for Elton. Though it had a first-rate collection of songs by Phil Cody, Howie Greenfield and me, I knew from the day of its release that it was going to bomb out. I could sense the lack of enthusiasm from Elton and Rocket Records. When Gerald Edelstein, my lawyer, and Elliott Abbott, my manager, tried to renegotiate a new contract for me, they were told, "Neil should be indebted to us for launching his second career." I was indebted, but I also felt that my hit records had put Rocket Records on the map. I demanded a better deal if I was to continue with them.

Elton and his company refused to offer any substantial amount of money to me or promotion for *Steppin' Out*. It was time to move on to another label. I signed with Elektra Records, distributed by Warner Brothers Communications.

I did meet Elton John several times after our split-up, and our meetings were cordial—but cold. It's something I'll always regret.

I had always thought that money could solve everything. But what good is it if you've lost the ability to relax and experience life as pleasure? I had never practiced moderation. There was always too much food and whiskey. The career was zooming but I was mired in obsessive worries. I found fault with everything. My creativity became a source of anguish. Being on the road forty weeks out of the year I started to write less and less. Because I was still afraid the bottom of my career would fall out, I pushed even harder. The stage became my only consolation—an unreal world of immediate applause and standing ovations. The most precious thing of all, peace of mind, eluded me.

The reviews started to turn. Critics complained I was taking my comeback for granted. Elton John warned me that once an artist becomes commercially accepted the reviewers turn sour. My reviews now depressed me deeply. I knew I was growing in leaps and bounds as a performer. Bad reviews not only upset me, I dwelled on them and took their poison with me to the next performance.

Critics were also harping on my weight and there, I'm afraid, they were right. I was fat as a house. I looked awful.

The piano became a symbol of fear. If I didn't write for a time, I felt sick and inadequate. Every time I

walked past the piano, it seemed to scream, "Neil, let's
see how good you really are. Are you afraid? Have you
run out of melodies?" Eventually, I stopped writing
every day. "How long do I have to prove my ability?" I
would try to convince myself. I would just write a
month or two before my new LP was to be recorded.
The songs usually turned out well, but it was much
more difficult than writing every day. When you write
daily your creative juices flow better. You use that part
of the brain that's so important for composing. After all
the hits, I couldn't face the chance of coming up with
something mediocre. Instead I concentrated on performing—a grave mistake, but the money on the road
was too good to turn down. I was now making up to
$50,000 a night and the concerts had gotten into my
bloodstream, the love of crowds, excitement, flowers in
the dressing room and adulation. It was a vicious, self-
destructive cycle. Finally I realized I had to write new
songs or I would no longer have any purpose in life.

Leba and I dreamed of having a co-op—something
we could own instead of just rent. I had fun looking at
all the beautiful places along Park Avenue and Fifth
Avenue. I did not imagine that I would have trouble
being accepted into the prestige buildings with open-
ings. You had to be screened by a building's board of
directors. I had two strikes against me, being Jewish
and a celebrity. The buildings were inhabited by old
moneyed people who did not relish the thought of au-
tograph seekers in front of their door. They were afraid
of wild parties and considered me to be an undesirable
occupant.

One by one, the buildings turned us down. It seemed our only alternatives were a town house or a move to Los Angeles. Leba was not anxious to live in a town house, and I would never be happy in L.A. Finally we decided to look at houses in Connecticut.

Joanne Woodward suggested a house in Westport, Connecticut. I felt a wonderful warmth and comfort in this house, perhaps because of its showbusiness history. Martha Raye had owned it for several years. David Wayne, the current owner, was renting it to Robert Redford.

I bought the house in 1977 and it's been home ever since.

CHAPTER 32
FAMILY TIES

Marc and Dara were almost grown now. They had been uprooted many times, changing schools and neighborhoods because of the peripatetic nature of the music business. I always treated them like adults, even when they were small. They thought of me not only as a father, but as a close friend. Maybe that's because I am a child at heart.

Marc and I roller skate together, play billiards, backgammon, and tennis. We fish and go on yachting trips together. He is even tempered and polite—something that's not always easy as the son of a celebrity. One day he asked, "Why did you have to be famous?" Kids had a tendency to single him out in school, and he was always a little embarrassed by my fame. People constantly ask him, "Do you sing too?" When a father is successful,

there is always extra pressure on the son. But Marc
takes it all in stride. I know he will be a winner at whatever he chooses to do.

Dara is the musical one. She started to write her own
songs at age nine. She had been born with a naturally
beautiful voice. I recorded two of her songs on my single records—"Hey Mr. Sunshine" and "Nana's Song."
Later she came with me on a concert tour of Japan to
sing background vocals. She was to be on many recordings of mine. I realize with Marc and Dara that I am
truly blessed.

And then there's Leba. At the end of the seventies
Leba said, "Why don't you buy back your publishing
catalogue from Don Kirshner. I think he might be willing to sell it for the right price." She thought it would
be a great annuity. Instead of having just the writing
royalties, I would make twice as much as writer and
publisher. The idea appealed to me, but I was a bit
doubtful about owning and running a publishing firm.
After much negotiation, I paid $2 million for the cata-
logue.

I was a publisher for one year, something I enjoyed
enormously. But it just took too much time away from
performing and writing. The publishing business is a
full-time job. When I decided to sell, there were several
offers, and finally Saul Steinberg offered me $3.5 mil-
lion for the catalogue. It seemed a pretty good profit for
a year.

In 1980 Dara and I cut a record together, "Should
Have Never Let You Go." Now Dara learned what it
was like to sweat out the charts. We went everywhere

promoting the record together and when I introduced
Dara to live audiences, I said "For me, as a father, this
is the ultimate *kvell*."

Poor Leba, who had been handling my management
after a parting of the ways with Elliott Abbott, now
had two stars to contend with.

We watched the record climb to the Top Twenty on
the national charts.

During a summer tour, I woke up with severe pains
in my lower stomach. If I had not had my appendix out
at age five, I would have sworn it was appendicitis. I
had to cancel the tour and fly to see Baruch Kodsi, an
old friend and head of gastroenterology at Maimonides
Hospital in Brooklyn. I had a condition called diverticulitis—small pockets in the intestines which were in-
flamed. I was put in the hospital for a week and had to
be fed intravenously. Too many years of eating improp-
erly—too much grease, fried foods, whiskey, wine, and
midnight snacks—had caught up with me. Baruch explained that this was a warning. I had to change my
ways and learn the art of moderation.

Over several months, I dieted away forty-one
pounds. My waist went from thirty-eight inches to
thirty-one. I've been able to maintain my weight ever
since then. I weigh myself every day before I eat breakfast. I like to stay between 135 and 138 pounds. If I find
I am 139, I eat very little that day to lose the extra
pound. The same thing goes for 134—I'll eat a little
more to gain the pound. The body is like a fine instrument that must be tuned correctly. I do situps every

day, plus jumping rope. I also have frequent body massages.

My breakfast is always the same: orange juice, decaffeinated coffee, toast with a little margarine, and a bowl of bran flakes with skim milk. My lunch is always one of two choices: either a fruit platter with cottage cheese or a grilled cheese sandwich with a green vegetable. I never eat between meals. My treat is one vodka on the rocks at cocktail time. My dinner is always variations on the same four or five items; I never look at a menu in a restaurant. I order a half-dozen raw oysters or clams, a small mixed salad with oil and vinegar on the side and a piece of broiled fish or chicken or a veal chop with rice or mashed potatoes—no gravy ever— and a green vegetable. Dessert is a small vanilla ice cream.

In an Italian restaurant I have a small fettucini Alfredo (easy on the cream and butter). Usually I leave some on my plate and then have a veal piccato entree. In a Chinese restaurant I order spare ribs and shrimp with lobster sauce (no onions because of my digestive condition). In a Japanese restaurant I begin with sashimi (raw fish), then chicken terriyaki and white rice. In a French restaurant I have smoked salmon and then duck with orange sauce. I never eat Mexican, Indian or other spicy foods. I never have mustard, pepper, nuts, onions, ketchup, franks, coffee, or butter and garlic sauces. This is because of my diverticulitis. Once in a great while I eat steak or roast beef. I have two or three glasses of wine with dinner, always accompanied by at least three glasses of water. This fills me up and sub-

stitutes for drinking too much wine. My soft drink is
Diet 7-Up.

I'm not saying this diet will work for everyone, but it
has kept me between 135–138 for the last two years. I
must admit to being something of a masochist. I sometimes almost enjoy hunger pains as they signify progress toward a goal. The key to my fitness is moderation,
plus eating the same foods—and weighing in every day.

In 1977, as I celebrated my twenty-fifth year as a
songwriter, Leba decided to throw a surprise party at
Regine's in New York, a kind of "This Is Your Life."
Apparently, she had made a mental note of all the
stories and names from my past. She and my secretary,
Sue Brownlees, got together and contacted every-
one, including my first girlfriend from Camp Echo
Lake, Ellen Burland; Edgar Roberts, my first piano
teacher; Mrs. Eisen, my choral instructor from Lincoln
High School; Mr. Goldman, the music instructor in
Lincoln; The Nordanels; the Gershons; The Tokens;
Hank Medress; Jay Siegel; and Cynthia Zolotin. There
were musicians, arrangers and conductors, friends from
3260 Coney Island Avenue—Leba didn't forget a soul.
The party was a great success. I felt I had accomplished
something over the twenty five years.

CHAPTER 33

PICTURES FROM THE PAST

I was with Mac and Eleanor Sedaka one day in December of 1980 on the golf course when Mac scored a hole in one. When Mother complimented him, he grabbed her and gave her a long, passionate kiss that had bystanders gaping. Mac was sixty-seven years old.

"Mac," Eleanor said, "you have been a loving husband to me for forty-six years."

Mac winked at me and said, "Nothing's too good for our Skinny, right, Neil? She didn't wait for Women's Lib."

Later I got a call from my mother from the doctor's office in Ft. Lauderdale. They feared my father had a tumor in his colon.

I immediately flew him to the Sloan Kettering Institute in New York where he was operated on two days later, on January sixth. After the operation the surgeon

came out and said to the gathered clan, "Some days you
are a good surgeon. Some days you're lucky. Today I
was both."

Dara, Marc, Eleanor, Leba, Ronnie, Gary and Barry
were leaping with joy around Poppa's bed when he
came out of the anaesthesia. I broke out the champagne
and gave Mac the good news that the operation was a
success and he was going to be okay. The first words he
uttered were, "I want to go home to Florida, Skinny."
Then he recognized his grandchildren and said,
"When's our next bowling match? I'm going to beat the
socks off everyone."

He was so glad for this reprieve, this man who had discovered the secret of happiness within his own being.

Between gigs now I would go to Ft. Lauderdale with
the family to spend as much time as possible with Mac
as he recuperated from his operation. The children and
Leba tried to get down as often as possible on weekends
to be with him. We were sitting on his patio having a
beer at sunset one day when I suddenly found myself
confiding my deepest anxieties to Dad.

"It's like I've always been on a roller coaster. When
will those up and down rides stop and when can I begin
really enjoying the ride? I worry about my next
hit . . . I worry about my throat . . . I can't enjoy going
dancing for fear of catching a draft : . . or go walking for
fear of catching a cold. And now I can't even enjoy eating."

"Neil," Dad said to me, "you know my philosophy
of life—I have always tried to keep things as uncompli-
cated for myself as possible. Enjoy each day as if it is a
gift. If you are not hurting anyone, do what you want

in that day." Mac had lived more in his sixty seven years than most people. He had a great joy for life. He could appreciate life to its fullest.

As soon as Mac was able to stand and get around a bit, he insisted that his grandchildren take him bowling. At the bowling alley that night, it was standing room only as all Mac's family and Florida friends cheered him on to a sensational victory. The kids blew the match to let him win. Mac was jubilant but it had been a mistake to go bowling so soon after the operation. He collapsed on the floor.

The surgeon who had been proud after the operation had not in fact been so lucky after all. Cancer of the colon had spread to the bones. After that, it goes fast.

Mac refused to be hospitalized again and I arranged for nurses around the clock so he could come home. Leba and Ronnie were staying with him as the doctor had warned us he could go at any moment. Frail as he was, no one could keep him in bed.

I was singing at Harrah's in Reno but kept in constant touch with Leba. When she told me how bad it was I cut short the engagement and flew to Ft. Lauderdale. My mother told Dad, "Neil is coming Thursday. If you don't lie down I won't let him come."

When I arrived Dad was sinking into a coma and my nephew Gary was screaming, "Poppa! Poppa! Don't go away!"

He raised himself up in the bed and managed to wink at them. Then he saw me and said, "Why Neil, you're home."

Then he began to sink again and Gary and Barry ran

to the bed yelling, "Poppa, don't! Poppa, please!"

The nurse looked at me and said, "You know, they should let him go, Mr. Sedaka. Otherwise, we are going to have to bring in the life-support equipment."

Leba joined us around his bed and reminded Mac of the role he'd played in our marriage. When Leba had first met me, it was Mac who kept up a correspondence with her, as he had with many fans around the world, using my name as Cyrano de Bergerac had done for Christian and Roxanne.

Exhausted from the flight from Reno, I finally went to bed. I'd expected to sleep for hours but, oddly, I woke at 6 A.M.

I went into Dad's bedroom and took him in my arms. He was in a coma now and the nurse was shaking her head slowly when I looked up at her in grief.

"I want to say something to him," I said to her, not knowing what could be said now.

"Go ahead," she said. "The last thing to go is the hearing, even in a coma."

I heard myself singing "Pictures From the Past" to him, his favorite song.

It was June 6, 1981. Mac Sedaka opened his eyes and looked at me, totally alert, and then he closed his eyes, forever.

I was vaguely aware of someone in the doorway. I turned and saw that is was Mom. We comforted each other and have continued to do so ever since.

Mom and I had always had a warm and special relationship over the years. I don't think any mother and son could be closer than we had become. I adore her and will never forget all the sacrifices she made for me.

EPILOGUE

Life has been good to me. I think dealing with people in a positive way has helped. People, I believe, are basically good. This trust, compassion for people, has always pulled me through even during the years of lonely obscurity when my record sales had plummeted and people had forgotten my name. I've never really changed as a result of the fame, the money. I try to surround myself with the people I love, the people who give me happiness.

For my talent, I am very grateful. Because of my talent, I feel in turn I must leave something to remain on earth after I'm gone. My music is a gift. Leaving something that makes people happy is what my career has been all about.

APPENDIXES

NEIL SEDAKA
ALBUM
DISCOGRAPHY

.

YEAR	TITLE	RECORD LABEL	CATALOG #
1958	*Neil Sedaka and The Tokens*	Guest Star	G1448
1958	*Neil Sedaka and The Tokens & Coins*	Crown Records	CST 641
1959	*Neil Sedaka*	RCA Victor	LPM 2035
1961	*Circulate*	RCA Victor	LSP 2317
1963	*Nuestro Neil Sedaka en Español*	RCA-Spain	
1964	*Mas Neil Sedaka en Español*	RCA-Spain	
1964	*Neil Sedaka Italiano*	RCA-Italy	

245

YEAR	TITLE	RECORD LABEL	CATALOG #
1965	Neil Sedaka Italiano Vol. 2	RCA-Italy	
1965	Smile	RCA-Italy	
1970	On Stage	RCA Camden-England	
1971	Emergence	RCA	APL1-1789
1972	Yesterday's Pop Scene	RCA-Belgium	
1972	Solitaire	RCA	APL1-1790
1973	The Tra La Days Are Over	MGM	2315-248
1974	The Neil Sedaka Collection	RCA-Belgium	
1974	Gold Deluxe	RCA-Japan	
1974	Sedaka's Back	Rocket	MCA 463
1974	I Go Ape	RCA	LJL1 7517
1974	Laughter in the Rain	Polydor	2383-265 super
1974	Neil Sedaka Live at the Royal Festival Hall	Polydor	2383-299
1975	24 Rock 'n' Roll Hits	RCA Starcall	HY 1005
1975	Oh Carol & Other Big Hits	RCA	ANL1 0879
1975	Overnight Success	Polydor	2442 131
1975	Neil Sedaka Sings His Greatest Hits	RCA	APL1 0928
1975	The Hungry Years	Rocket	PIG 2157
1975	Neil Sedaka Original Hits	RCA	DPL2 0149
1975	Let's Go Steady Again	RCA Camden	CDS 1151
1976	Stupid Cupid	RCA Camden	CDS 1147

YEAR	TITLE	RECORD LABEL	CATALOG #
1976	*Breaking Up Is Hard to Do—The Original Hit*	Pickwick	ACL 7006
1976	*Pure Gold*	RCA	ANL1 1314
1976	*Laughter and Tears*	Polydor	2383 399
1976	*Live in Australia*	RCA	VPL1 1540
1976	*Neil Sedaka on Stage*	RCA Camden	
1976	*Steppin' Out*	Rocket	PIG 2195
1977	*Neil Sedaka's Greatest Hits*	Rocket	PIG 2297
1977	*Sedaka The '50s & '60s*	RCA	APL1 2254(e)
1977	*Neil Sedaka & Songs—A Solo Concert*	Polydor	2672 036
1977	*Sounds of Sedaka*	MCA	MCF 2780
1977	*A Song*	Elektra	6E-102
1978	*The Many Sides of Neil Sedaka*	RCA	AFL1 2524
1978	*All You Need Is the Music*	Elektra	6E-161
1980	*In the Pocket*	Elektra	6E-259
1981	*Neil Sedaka—Now*	Elektra	6E-348

THE SONGS OF NEIL SEDAKA

(a partial list)

"A Little Bit Older (A Little Bit Wiser)"
"A Little Lovin' "
"A Synonym of Tears and Rain"
"Adam and Eve"
"The Adventures of a Boy Child Wonder"
"Alice in Wonderland"
"All I Need Is You"
"All the Words in the World"
"All You Need Is the Music"
"Alone at Last"
"Alone in New York"
"Amarillo"
"Another Day Another Heartache"
"Another Sleepless Night"
"The Answer Lies Within"
"Anywhere You're Gonna Be (Leba's Song)"
"As Long as I Live"
"Baby Blue"
"Baby Roo"
"Bad Blood"
"Bad Bad Scene"
"Bad Girl"

"Be There Baby"
"Beautiful You"
"Better Days Are Coming"
"Betty Grable"
"The Big Parade"
"Born to Be Bad"
"Bouncin' All Over the World"
"Breaking Up Is Hard to Do"
"Brief Season"
"Bring Me Down Slow"
"Calendar Girl"
"Candy Kisses"
"Cardboard California"
"Caribbean Rainbow"
"Cellophane Disguise"
"Chippewa Town"
"Circulate"
"City Boy"
"The Clock Has No Hands"
"The Closest Thing to Heaven"
"Comin' Home to Stay"
"Cowboys and Indians"
"Crossroads"
"Crying My Heart Out for You"
"The Diary"
"Dimbo Man"
"Do It Like You Done It When You Meant It"
"Don't Be Too Good to My Baby"
"Don't Hide Your Love"
"Don't Lead Me On"
"Don't Let It Mess Your Mind"
"Don't Look Over Your Shoulder"
"Don't Turn Around"
"Dreamland"
"Ebony Angel"
"Electric Mirror"
"Endlessly"
"ESP"
"Everybody's Got Hot Pants"
"Express Yourself"
"The Face of Love"
"Fallin' "
"Fallin in Love Again" (a.k.a. "Here We Are Falling in Love Again")
"First Taste of Romance"
"Flame"
"For Only Those in Love"
"For the Good of the Cause (Times Square Boogie)"
"Forget Her"
"Frankie"
"Georgia Road"
"Getting Back to Nature"
"The Girl I Left Behind Me"
"God Bless Joanna"
"God Save America"
"Goin' Home to Mary Lou"
"Going Nowhere"
"Gone with the Morning"

"Good Times, Good Music,
Good Friends"
"Goodman Goodbye"
"Grown Up Games"
"The Gypsy Told Me So"
"Happy Birthday, Sweet
Sixteen"
"Happy New Year, Baby"
"Heartbreak House for
Homeless Children"
"Here Comes the Bride"
"His Kind of Woman"
"Hollywood Lady"
"Home"
"Hot and Sultry Nights"
"The Hungry Years"
"I Ain't Hurtin' No More"
"I Belong to You"
"I Don't Know What I Like
About You"
"I Found My World in
You"
"I Go Ape"
"I Hope He Breaks Your
Heart"
"I Let You Walk Away"
"I Must Be Dreaming"
"I Waited Too Long"
"If I Could Write a Song"
"If You Wanna Tell Your
Baby"
"I'm a Song (Sing Me)"
"I'm Gonna Wish for You"
"I'm No Good for You
Baby"
"The Immigrant"

"In a World of My Own"
"Is Anybody Gonna Miss
You"
"It Hurts to Be in Love"
"It Takes a Man to Make a
Woman"
"It's Good to Be Alive
Again"
"I've Never Really Been in
Love Before"
"Jeannine"
"Johnnie Walker, Old Gran-
dad, Jack Daniels and
You"
"Junkie for Your Love"
"Just Before Long"
"Keep a Walkin' "
"Keepin' My Eye on You"
"Kiddio (Go Try and Find
a Rainbow)"
"King of Clowns"
"Laughter in the Rain"
"The Leaving Game"
"Let Mama Know" (a.k.a.
"Let Daddy Know")
"Let the Good Times In"
"Let the People Talk"
"Letting Go"
"Let's Fall in Love To-
night"
"Let's Go Steady Again"
"Let's Go Where the Good
Times Go"
"Let's Make the Most of a
Beautiful Thing"
"Lightning Ridge"

"Like a Clinging Vine"
"Little Brother"
"Little Devil"
"Little Song"
"Lonely Night (Angel Face)"
"Losing You"
"Love Ain't an Easy Thing"
"Love in the Shadows"
"Love Is Spreading Over the World"
"Love Keeps Getting Stronger Every Day"
"Love Will Keep Us Together"
"Magic Colors"
"Make the Music Play"
"Make Your Own Sunshine" (a.k.a. "You Gotta Make Your Own Sunshine")
"Marathon Mary"
"Mediterranean Moonlight"
"The Miracle of You"
"Mister Saxophone"
"Moon of Gold"
"My Best Friend Barbara"
"My Friend"
"My Friend the Rain"
"My Kind of Woman"
"My One and Only Prayer to You and Only You"
"My World Keeps Getting Smaller Every Day"

"My World Is Slipping Away"
"Never Noticed It Before"
"New York City Blues"
"Next Door to an Angel"
"Nothing Less Than Forever"
"No Vacancy"
"Now and Then"
"Number One with a Heartache"
"Ocean Full of Teardrops"
"Oh Carol"
"On the Road Again"
"On the Outside Looking In"
"One Day in Your Life"
"One Little Smile"
"One More Mountain to Climb"
"One Night Stand"
"One Woman Man"
"Ooh Sha-La-La"
"The Other Side of Me"
"Pearl Divers Song"
"A Penny for Your Thoughts"
"Perfect Strangers"
"Pictures from the Past"
"Pictures in the Wine"
"Plastic Dreams and Toy Balloons"
"Pot of Gold"
"Puppet Man"
"Put a Little Meat on your Bones Lucinda"

"Put Out the Fire"
"The Queen of 1964"
"Rainy Day Bells"
"Rainy Jane"
"Rance Man"
"Right or Wrong"
"Ring Around Rosie"
"River Queen"
"Rollin' Out the Good
    Times"
"Rosemary Blue"
"Run Around"
"Run, Samson, Run"
"Sad Eyes"
"Sad, Sad Story"
"The Same Old Fool"
"Saturday Prom"
"School Girl" (a.k.a. "Rock
    'n' Roll Wedding Day")
"She Really Needs Me"
"She'll Never Be You"
"She's My Desire"
"Should've Never Let You
    Go"
"Silent Movies"
"Since You've Been Gone"
"Six Day Sinner"
"Sleeping Beauty"
"Sleazy Love"
"Slow Lovin' Man"
"Sogno d'Oro"
"Solitaire"
"Something Worth Waiting
    For"
"Somewhere"

"Stairway to Heaven"
"Standing on the Inside"
"Star Crossed Lovers"
"Stayin' Power"
"Steppin' Out"
"Stephen"
"Strangers in the Moon-
    light"
"Stupid Cupid"
"Sugar"
"Summertime Madness"
"Summer Nights"
"Summer Symphony"
"Sunny"
"Sunrise"
"Sushine Rose"
"Sunshine Rose"
"Superbird"
"Suspicions"
"Take Me to Your Heart"
"Teach Me How"
"Teenage Tears"
"That's When the Music
    Takes Me"
"This Endless Night"
"This Is Not Goodbye"
"This Is Not My Town"
"Tillie the Twirler"
"Time Marches On"
"Time Waits for No One"
"Time Will Tell"
"Tin Pan Alley"
"Tit for Tat"
"Today Is Shelby's Birth-
    day"